The Golden Fleece and Alchemy

SUNY Series in
Western Esoteric Traditions

David Appelbaum, Editor

The Golden Fleece and Alchemy

Antoine Faivre

STATE UNIVERSITY OF NEW YORK PRESS

Production by Ruth Fisher
Marketing by Lynne Lekakis

Published by
State University of New York Press, Albany

© 1993   State University of New York

For information, address the State University of New York Press,
State University Plaza, Albany, NY 12246

Library of Congress Cataloging-in-Publication Data

Faivre, Antoine, 1934-
  [Toison d'or et alchimie. English]
  The golden fleece and alchemy / Antoine Faivre.
      p.   cm. — (SUNY series in western esoteric traditions)
  Translation of: Toison d'or et alchimie, Paris-Milano, Archè, 1990.
  Includes bibliographical references and index.
  ISBN 0-7914-1409-4 (alk. paper). — ISBN 0-7914-1410-8 (pbk. :
alk,. paper)
  1. Argonauts (Greek mythology)   2. Alchemy.   I. Title.
II. Series
BL820. A8F3513   1993
292.1′3—dc20   92-5770
                                                         CIP

10 9 8 7 6 5 4 3 2 1

Mytholusitaniano pictori,
Figuratarum sacrarumque geometriarum
explanandarum experito,
Per Odysseos similes vias duci nostro,

LIMA DE FREITAS,

Hunc dedico libellum,
Promontorio Sacro susceptum,
Illius illuminatum operibus
Fervidaque fotum amicitia.

Contents

Table of Illustrations

Foreword

By Joscelyn Godwin

There is surely no subject as disconcerting to the rational mind as alchemy. Not only is the supposed transmutation of metals an insult to the empirical intelligence, but the writings of the alchemists seem calculated to tease and confuse, while their secretive arrogance does not inspire confidence in their pretended wisdom. More than any of the so-called occult sciences (astrology, Cabala, ceremonial magic, divination, etc.), alchemy evades definition. Being the science of correspondences between the different levels of being, it cannot be pinned down on any one level, least of all that of empirical experience and logical explanation. Like a serpent, or like the element of Mercury, alchemy slithers from the spiritual to the astral, from the etheric to the physical, and back again. Few indeed are those able to follow it in its peregrinations. In the most heroic attempt of modern times, C. G. Jung did his best to anchor it at the psychic level, but only at the expense of ignoring what most alchemists have been doing for two millenia and more: working in laboratories. Yet today's laboratory chemists are bound by a world view that has no room for intercourse between the levels of being—of which they acknowledge but one; thus, they can only regard alchemy as the distant, cranky ancestor of their own science.

If we are to understand why so many people have thought fit to spend their time and resources on the pursuit of alchemy—assuming that they were not much more foolish than ourselves—then there is a formidable amount of research to be done. Compared with subjects like the history of art, or of religion, that of alchemy has scarcely begun. What studies there have been tend to treat the influence of alchemy on something else, which is interesting and often surprising, but which does not bring one much closer to the Royal Art itself.

On first sight, Antoine Faivre's book on the Golden Fleece appears to be a scholarly study of one alchemical theme, treated historically.

1

This appearance is deceptive, however. Certainly his laboratory is that of the scholar, equipped with all the necessary apparatus: he is a Germanist by training, a veteran of the Eranos Conferences, and a Professor at the Sorbonne. But more than that, this is an example of someone actually working alchemically. Faivre takes as his First Matter the image of the Golden Fleece, and works on it with all the resources of erudition. The book itself is a voyage—an Argosy—through the Western imagination, led by a guide who points out the curious landmarks that betray the imprint of this particular myth. These tend to involve a link between the physical world and another level of being. For example, the collar of the fifteenth-century Order of the Golden Fleece consists of golden links joined by flintstones: the mineral in which the spark of fire lies latent. Can one imagine the frame of mind of whoever designed and approved such a curious and evidently magical combination? Elsewhere we learn of the power of sheep's wool to attract gold, filtering it out of aurific streams; but the German writer Fictuld suggests that it is rather a case of "astral gold," which in the springtime sign of the Ram enters the earth out of *Spiritus Mundi.* Others state that the fleece in question was a sheepskin parchment, containing the secrets of alchemy written in golden letters; or that the whole apparatus of Greek mythology existed solely to encode the secrets of the Royal Art.

Again, the sacrifice of the Ram or Lamb brings up a wealth of mythical imagery. In the "criobolium" ceremony of Antiquity, the initiate was literally bathed in its blood. whereas Christians are only figuratively "washed in the blood of the Lamb." There is a pervasive feeling that the blood, or, less repulsively to our taste, the hides of animals have some magical efficacy, varying according to the nature of the beast. The parchment that covers a shaman's drum is believed to incorporate the spirit of the sacrificed creature. Yogis are instructed to meditate seated on deer- or tiger-skins. Sufis wear only clothes of sheep's wool. And shamans, yogis, and Sufis all flourished in that region of Central Asia to which Colchis, on the Black Sea, is a doorway.

The myth of the Golden Fleece is the thread on which these and innumerable other images are strung. Erudition and scholarship are the controlling elements that prevent such a stringing from getting out of hand, as all too often occurs in the work of occultists. Yet the string is real enough, at least to the host of authors to which Faivre introduces us, who have been moved to fashion their works around this mythic image. Who should ever have suspected that it was so much alive—that alchemy itself was so vigorous—in early eighteenth-century Germany? Only those who appreciate that *The Magic Flute, The Disciples of Sais,* or the second part of *Faust* are not adventitious growths, but rooted firmly in the soil of the Germanic imagination. Again, how many Romance scholars realize the influence of alchemy on French culture? Only those who have happened to read the elegant but exasperating Fulcanelli and his disciple (or alter ego) Canseliet, whose wordplay and pseudoetymologies are central to the French tradition of esoteric entertainments, from Rabelais to Derrida.

Alchemy teaches us that the world is deeper than the daylight knowledge of reductionist thinking would like to make it. A scholarship limited to that kind of thinking is impotent when faced with the dusky ramifications of alchemical myth. Antoine Faivre shows that the road to mythical understanding lies through the Imagination. It must be emphasized that this Imagination (deliberately capitalized) is not the same as the "phantasy," a mental function often loosely identified with it. The Imagination is an organ of the mind that gives access, as the sense organs do, to a particular world of events and entities that take the form of images. These may or may not correspond to things seen in the external world; for instance, the Unicorn does not, nor does the Angel, unless we are Blake or Swedenborg. But they are real, not merely "imaginary." Those whose reality resides only in the external, physical world are welcome to the burden of explaining why people have lived or died for the sake of such images, and why Homer, Virgil, Dante, Shakespeare, and Goethe have given their best efforts to describing events in the world of the mythic Imagination. The extraordinary claim of alchemy is that the internal, mythic image and the external substance are in some way linked, so that transmutation may occur on both levels.

Faivre's exploration of the mythic images and events gathered in the Golden Fleece legend is controlled by the intellect, but not limited by it, any more than the meaning of a piece of music is limited to the mathematical relationships that control the notes. His work also shows that the study of an alchemical myth leads not merely to information, nor even just to knowledge, but, if one dare say so, to wisdom. With the publication this year of three of his books in English translation (the others are a study of the mythic figure of Hermes Trismegistus [Phanes Press] and a survey of the Western esoteric tradition [SUNY Press]), English language readers have a further opportunity to explore this vein of scholarship, which has been represented up to now mainly by Faivre's great predecessor at the Sorbonne, Henry Corbin.

It may be helpful if this Foreword concludes with an informal retelling of the myth in question. The many variants, subplots, and sources can be found in collections such as Robert Graves's *The Greek Myths*. (Harmondsworth: Penguin Books, 1960). Here I will select only the names and incidents essential to the present book.

THE MYTH OF THE GOLDEN FLEECE

Athamas was king of Boeotia in Greece, and his queen was Nephele, a phantom-woman created by Zeus in the form of the goddess Hera. Their sons were Phrixos and Leucon, their daughter Helle. In time, Athamas fell in love with another woman, Ino, whose parents were Cadmus and Harmonia. Out of jealousy against her predecessor, Ino contrived to persuade Athamas that he must placate the gods by sacrificing his son Phrixos. Athamas duly took his children up to a mountaintop, but just as he was about to kill his son, Heracles and the Olympian gods intervened. Hermes sent down a golden, winged ram called Chrysomellos, which carried off Phrixos and Helle on its back. Helle fell off into the sea at what is now called the "Hellespont," but Phrixos survived to reach Colchis, on the eastern shores of the Black Sea. Obedient to the gods, he sacrificed the miraculous ram and hung up its golden fleece on an oak tree in the sacred grove of Ares, guarded by a fearful dragon. There he lived, married, and died in exile; but no one performed the proper funeral rites for him.

The ghost of Phrixos came back to Greece to haunt Pelias, king of Iolchus, who had usurped the throne from his half-brother Aeson. Pelias had killed nearly all his rivals, but Aeson's son Jason, whom he thought stillborn, had escaped him. Jason was reared by Cheiron the wise centaur, and grew up to confront his wicked uncle and reclaim his rightful throne. Pelias consented, on condition that Jason would first go to Colchis, fetch the Golden Fleece, and lay the ghost of Phrixos to rest, thus restoring prosperity to Iolchus.

Jason accepted the quest, and assembled a distinguished host to man his ship, the *Argo:* it included the demigods Heracles and Orpheus, Castor and Polydeuces the Dioscuri, Calais and Zetes, sons of the North Wind, and many other famous heroes. Athena provided a piece of oak from the grove of Zeus at Dodona that could talk and prophesy, and this was set in the prow.

The first call of the Argonauts was at Lemnos, where they found the city populated only by women. Apparently the Lemnian men had complained that their wives stank, for which the women murdered them. The Argonauts were only too pleased to oblige the lonely widows and provide them with heirs: Jason himself took Hypsipyle, the Lemnian queen, and begot Euneus, who grew up to become their king. It took Hercules's club to rouse the heroes from their beds and send them back to their oars. But Hercules himself abandoned the quest when he lost his young friend Hylas in the woods.

Among their many adventures as they headed towards the Bosphorus was the encounter with Phineus, son of Agenor. King Phineus was being plagued by harpies that stole and fouled his food, so that he was at the point of starving to death. Calais and Zetes drove off the monsters and earned Phineus's gratitude, for which he told the Argonauts how to negotiate the coming peril. This was the Symplegades, clashing rocks that guarded the Bosphorus and crushed any ship that attempted to pass. On Phineus's advice, the Argonauts first let fly a bird, whose tail-feathers were clipped by the rocks as she passed; then, as the rocks withdrew, the Argo was rowed through at top speed, and lost only her stern ornament. Once outwitted, the magical Sympegades remained forever impotent, and the way to the Black Sea open.

At last they came to Colchis, at the opposite end of the Black Sea beneath the Caucasus Mountains. The ruler was King Aeëtes, whose daughter had married the exiled Phrixos. Naturally he did not want to surrender the Fleece, but Hera and Athena, Jason's Olympian patrons, contrived to have the king's other daughter, Medea, fall in love with the hero. Medea was a sorceress, and she promised to help Jason faithfully so long as he would make her his wife. He in turn swore by the the Olympian gods that he would remain faithful to her forever.

Aeëtes now agreed to surrender the Golden Fleece on the absurd condition that Jason could yoke his fire-breathing bulls, plow a field with them, and sow it with serpent's teeth. But with Medea's help the bulls were tamed, and, just as had happened to Cadmus, the teeth sprouted into a host of warriors. Jason provoked them into fighting each other to the death. and his task was done. But Aeëtes did not keep his part of the bargain. It took Medea's cunning and cold blood—for she connived at the murder and dismemberment of her own half brother, Aspyrtus—for the Argonauts to escape Colchis with their prize.

Defiled with murder, Jason and Medea could not continue with the ship, but went ashore at the island of Circe to be purified of their crime. After they had rejoined the Argonauts, many adventures befell them before they returned home to Iolchus. Here they learned that Pelias had killed Jason's parents and their little son. Rather than stage an attack on the city, however, Jason and Medea resorted to trickery. She visited the court of Pelias in the guise of an old crone, and promised the aged king that she could make him young again. For proof, she herself resumed her youthful form. "How was it to be done?" asked Pelias. To demonstrate, Medea had an old ram cut into thirteen pieces and boiled in a cauldron; then, by a conjuring trick, she produced a young lamb. The king consented to the same treatment, which was dutifully carried out by his own daughters; and that was the end of him.

Jason dedicated the Golden Fleece in the temple of Laphystian

Zeus, then went with Medea to rule Corinth, where she had inherited the throne. Later, believing that she had secured the succession through murder, he proposed to divorce her and marry another woman, Glauce. The vengeful Medea sent an inflammable robe as a wedding-gift, which resulted in a fire that killed Glauce and everyone present, including King Creon of Thebes; Jason alone escaped. Nevertheless, the gods continued to favor Medea, whose glamorous career took her to Athens and Colchis before she attained immortality in Elysium. But Jason had forfeited their support when he broke his oath of fidelity, and was left to the life of a penniless wanderer. In old age he returned to Corinth, where the *Argo* was still beached, and sat beneath the prow of his old flagship. Thereupon the piece of oracular oak fell on his head and killed him. The *Argo* itself took its place among the stars, where it can still be seen.

Introduction

This little book has its origins in the confluence of three themes which are related to a special occasion.

The first theme is that of the philosophers' stone, hidden within a pictorial puzzle. It occurs repeatedly throughout Dom Pernety's book *Les Fables égyptiennes et grecques dévoilées et réduites au même principe* (Paris, 1758). In 1982, the Editions de la Table d'Emeraude issued a facsimile of the book (1786 edition), prefaced by an original study authored by Sylvain Matton and entitled "L'herméneutique alchimique de la Fable antique" (21 pages). As far as I know, this fine exposition seems to be the first treatment of the subject not confined to one particular point. Here Matton deals with the efforts of those ancient scholars striving to establish that the secrets of the Great Work would have been deliberately concealed behind the veil of purely mythological motifs and characters. His investigation starts with Byzantine authors and goes up to the Renaissance (in the broad sense of the term), as studied through Latin and French writings. These scholars present two different, and even conflicting, aspects. The first seeks to find only one possible translation for a myth or an image: a reductionist approach, since it ignores the fact that neither domain—myth or alchemy—can be forced into any word-for-word equivalents. Interestingly, however, adepts have never been found wanting who were so fond of spirituality, of initiatory and symbolic journeys, as to wish—like Dom Pernety, whose title is so explicit—to "reduce" fables to "one single principle." On the other hand, the second reading, practiced mostly from the early seventeenth century onwards, breaks the shackles of unidimensional allegorism, turning into brilliant hermeneutics and blossoming into open discourses with much poetry and theosophy.

The second theme is that of a message inscribed on a mythic object. This message is all the more cryptic or pregnant with a variety of meanings as its medium is more deeply immersed in a fantastic tale. This theme is embedded in various motifs. Thus, the tomb of C. R-C, in the

Rosicrucian *Fama* of 1614, is covered with inscriptions inviting glosses, or some form of gnosis. Or, similarly, the Emerald Tablet bearing the cryptic and famous text of that name. For the past five years, part of my seminar (at the E.P.H.E.*, Sorbonne) has been devoted to many of the multi-leveled interpretations of this Tablet, and so I have seen how easily this second motif tends to overlap with a third—that of the Golden Fleece. The ram's skin carried Phrixos and Helle through the air, and to recover which Jason went to Colchis, has often been looked on as a parchment with an alchemical text written on it.

The third theme, that of the odyssey, is here connected with the town of Tomar, in Portugal; the title of the colloquium held there in 1986 sounded like an invitation to set off on a journey: *Odyssées réelles et Odyssées spirituelles (Actual Odysseys and spiritual Odysseys)*. Since I was asked to deliver a lecture, it came to me that I could connect this theme with the other two: that is, I could speak about the Golden Fleece in alchemy. The venture of the Argonauts, whether spiritual or imaginary, has left a definite trace in history, if only a chivalric Order which has the Golden Ram as its symbol! Exploring these texts, with a spiritual or scholarly or cultural purpose—this in itself may prove quite an odyssey.

The preparation of a thirty-minute talk prompted me to go ahead with my investigations and reflections. All the more so, since the Emerald Tablet—a topic that was to remain for a long time on my agenda—again and again conjured up before me the golden ram. Then the time came for connecting the still scattered material, and this earlier than expected, for a special occasion, namely the preparation of a paper for the Alchemy Conference held at Groningen, Netherlands, in April 1989. The present study, written afterwards, has no claim to exhaustivity. Still, it is the first comprehensive study of the story of the Golden Fleece in alchemy, comprehensive in the sense that it is not restricted to one period, and also it introduces writings from the Germanic sphere.

The absence of material from the Anglo-Saxon world, and probably of some others as well, is a matter of regret. This was due not to a lack of interest, but to the unavailability of documents. Perhaps there was need for more searching and more patience. But an endless quest for exhaustivity can prevent scrupulous authors from sharing their findings.

The present work, which calls not only for comments but also for supplements, is therefore primarily intended to inspire researchers to further enlarge and elaborate on the material collected so far.

---

*Ecole Pratique des Hautes Études

From the Byzantines to the Rosicrucians

One among a set of long-standing issues concerns the origins of the myths. Is it possible to trace the emergence of the stories of the Trojan War, or of the foundation of Rome? Did all the gods, often so anchored on earth, have actual human models? First of all, who was Hermes Trismegistus: a sage and an initiate? Or some fictitious character based on the image of Thot-Hermes?[1] Who was Agenor? The son of a Phoenician hero? The composite of several actual but untraceable figures? Or a product of sheer imagination?

Like the Trismegistus, Agenor is a civilizing hero. He is said to have initiated mining and smelting, and invented, or at least exploited, the alphabet. As such, he is more 'real' than any historical figure, who would be credited with only some of these initiatives. Agenor, the Westerner, could easily bring us to Jason for his directing the migrating peoples westward, following the course of the sun.[2] Certainly Phrixos' ram, and then the Argonauts, start moving eastward, not westward, but here the main idea is that there be an *orientation*. Agenor's son, Cadmus (the name derives from *Kadmie,* philosophers' soil), an adept in chemistry, is also one of the architects of ancient civilization which, in our culture, is related to navigation. As a matter of fact, the Phoenicians were the first great navigators: the *Voyage of Hannon,* sixth century B.C., describes the exploration of the west African coast, down to the Rio del Ouro. However, it is with Jason that we begin the series of odysseys which have come down to us, at least in Europe. One well-established tradition even claims that this myth is one generation earlier than the myth of Ulysses.[3]

Although we will not describe here in detail the well-known adventures of Phrixos or the Argonauts, they can safely be seen as gravitating around two powerful archetypes: namely the journey to the East and what could be termed the "Holy Spirit Fire." Riding his ram, cleaving the air, Phrixos starts from Thebes and flies eastward to Colchis. This orientation may indeed correspond to migratory and trading movements which have left visible traces, but it may also correspond to an initiatory journey, a spiritual geography.[4] In any case, while there is no need to dwell on this well-known *topos,* the archetype of the "Feu Saint-Esprit" is, perhaps, less known.

The gold of the ram's skin gives us a clue. Playing with letters, we find that each letter of the name of the hero of the Fleece corresponds to the first letter of each of the most productive months of the year (July, August, September, October, November = JASON), and this fertility may be understood in a spiritual sense.[5] Prosaically as well as poetically, the Golden Fleece, whose Latin name is *aureum vellus,* is also *bractea viva* whenever it refers to the yellow fleece of the sheep of Hesperia; in Virgil, *bratta auri* means "golden leaf."[6] It is well known that gold is very often a symbol of light. As for the Iranian and Mazdaznan light of glory, or *xvarnah* (Avestian term), Henry Corbin reminds us that it is identical to the oriflamme (*orie-flambe*), golden flame (*flamme d'or*), or "flaming gold" (*qui flambe*).[7] This is a Zoroastrian notion used to refer to the "victorial fire," one visible aspect of which is the nimbus, the flame, or the *aurea gloria* which has for its symbol the *flammula,* the *orie flambe.* Such heavenly and primal radiance is found again as the halo of Christian saints. This light is itself an object of vision; it is that which enables us to see; it combines both the Greek notions of *doxa* (glory) and *tykhê* (fate).

The versatility of this image archetype allows us to draw parallels with the Golden Fleece. For one thing, we find here again the idea of a mythical Orient, for the *xvarnah,* in Iran, is also said to be a source of "oriental knowledge," or "knowledge of the Orientals" (*Isrâqîyûn*). For another, the Mazdaznan *xvarnah* appears at times as a ram. And if we accept, with Henry Corbin, that the *xvarnah* and the Holy Grail are one and the same representation,[8] we discover at the same time a relationship, or even an identity, between these two symbols and the symbol of the ram. One form of hypostasis of the *xvarnah,* in the earthly, historic world, is the light of glory of the Knights in the Iranian epic: they assembled around a light or a 'grail'. Thus a link between the image of the ram and chivalry is established long before Philip the Good brought them together when he founded his Order.[9]

Fond of pagan history, medieval literature is familiar with Jason's adventures and with his trophy: through Statius (*Thebais,* Book V), through Ovid's enduring success (*Metamorphoses,* Book VII, *Heroids,* parts VI and XII), and Dares the Phrygian, another late Latin writer who, in his *De Excidio Troiae historia,* a short account in prose, relates them to the Trojan history and takes our myth as a prelude to it. In this Dares is followed by Benoît de Sainte-Maure, whose *Roman de Troie* (circa 1165) is one of the most significant medieval works devoted to the story of Hector, Priam, and Helena.[10] Benoît, then, starts with the feat of Jason in Colchis. This is a prelude to the whole subsequent Trojan epic, containing in seed-form the epic's main themes. Moreover, describing the Golden Fleece at the beginning is to root the novel in origins unrelated to chronology, that is, in the *in illo tempore* of mythic space. And at the same time, the story of Jason becomes connected with fantasy and magic of an esoteric type, since it is a constant feature in the *Roman de Troie,* for instance, in the passage describing the 'Chamber of Beauties', with its automations, or rather its magic figures. The chamber obviously stands for knowledge of the world, stored here encyclopedically and symbolically in a mirror, emblematic of the one reflecting the whole universe.[11] And later, in the early fourteenth century, the famous *Ovide moralisé* contains perhaps the most comprehensive account of Jason, prior to Raoul Lefèvre's novel. Here the personage is equated with Christ. *Ovide moralisé* was a successful and enduring work. In addition, we may also mention Boccaccio's *De genealogia deorum,* where we find a long passage about the Argonauts; this book has been reedited and translated several times.[12] All the same, because it became an increasingly common practice to use the themes and motifs associated with the Golden Fleece, it seems that the Middle Ages were giving way to the Renaissance from the time of the fifteenth century.

It is probably no accident that the fifteenth century, an Odyssean era, saw the revival of the myth of the Golden Fleece. After the appalling fourteenth century, which witnessed the black plague, the great schism, religious disputes, and the destruction of the Order of the Temple, the collective imagination opened up spontaneously to brighter and wider vistas. In 1429, the son of John the Fearless, Philip the Good, Duke of

Burgundy, married the daughter of the King of Portugal. This marriage between the two countries was arranged with the help of a man sent by Philip on a special mission, Jan Van Eyck, who in 1425 had already gone into the service of the Duke as a painter and a member of his personal staff. He was sent with a group of diplomats to ask the King of Portugal, John the First, for the gift of his daughter Isabel in marriage. The year he married, Philip founded the chivalric Order of the Golden Fleece. It was also at this time than Jan Van Eyck and his brother Hubert painted the polyptych of *The Mystic Lamb*—a symbolic brother to the golden ram —completed in 1432 and now in Saint-Bavon cathedral, Ghent.

Elsewhere I have had the opportunity to discuss symbols and designs of the Order. Therefore, let us consider here the main if not the only, element relevant to our purpose: the collar which every knight is requested to wear. Allegedly producing invisible sparks, it consists of a gold chain made of eight links, each containing two steel flintstones and having a pendant clothed in the golden wool of the Fleece. This, of course, is the ram's fleece, but we must remember how the ram is still closely associated with the lamb. During the feast made on the founding day of the Order, a blue lamb with golden horns was presented: "a sheep, alive, painted blue, and with gilded horns." We will not elaborate here on the blue light, however significant, but it is noteworthy that the symbolism of this animal and that of the ram complement each other. *Agnos* means both "pure, saint" and "unknown, not known"; and, as René Alleau has pointed out, "the Greek 'agnus' was the name of the *stone* or stones that the weavers hung to their canvas in order to weave them."[13] So the stone hanging from the weaver's canvas and the ram hanging from the stone of the fire-giving collar come together in the image of the lamb, with the vivid symbolism of weaving, significant on both the macrocosmic and the microcosmic levels.

At the Court of Burgundy, this Fleece is not confined to the Order of that name. It is also found on tapestry: as early as 1393, Philip the Brave ordered two tapestries (which Philip the Good, therefore, could have seen in his early childhood); in 1448 he too ordered eight huge pieces of tapestry in Tournai, featuring the Fleece of Gedeon. But we find it first of all as a recurrent theme in literature. It appears for the first time in Jean Mausel's *Fleur des Histoires.* And around 1454, a minor allegorico-didactic work ascribed to Chastellain foreshadows later hermetic interpretations, for here Jason is taken as a symbol of the human body, while Hercules symbolizes the soul and Colchis the world. As for the Fleece, it "is the noble gift, an unsurpassable honor / that is within oneself, when one goes through the hardship of many obstacles / Above, in Heaven, in eternal glory."[14] Then comes Raoul Lefèvre, the most celebrated of the Golden Fleece novelists who, in 1456, wrote his *Histoire de Jason*. What is remarkable about it for us is that we find here both the Golden Fleece and the parchement of the 'emerald tablet' type. For here we learn that a king, called Apollo, received a parchment handwritten by the god Mars and containing "all the mysteries that should be observed and preserved to achieve such a lofty thing." This "lofty thing" is the Fleece. The parchment itself was handed down from generation to generation, until Medea gave it to Jason. Let us also mention Guillaume Fillastre, Chancellor of the Order and Bishop of Tournai. His *Thoison d'Or,* written between 1468 and 1473, prefigured the alchemical readings of this myth, even more than the two previous works.

Fillastre portrays Junon as our first mother who, because of her sin, shut off her children from heaven, so they roamed the world, struggling through an ocean of tribulations, in much the same way as Phrixos and Helle in the air. Indeed, this is the kind of ocean human beings often fall into, just like Helle, who was unable to remain firmly seated on the ram. Nevertheless, strong and unwavering beings are able to land on the isle of Colchis, to enter the temple of Jupiter—the Church, that is —where the Golden Fleece (our pure and saintly soul) is offered to God. Having killed the children from his first bed, Phineus is harassed by the Harpies; and his liberator, as we know, is Jason. According to Fillastre, Phineus means Adam who, for having listened to Eve, condemned all of us to death. The Harpies are the demons, Jason is Christ, Argo "the virginal womb of the glorious Virgin Mary," Medea is redeemed humanity, and the conquest of the Fleece the "redemption of the human lineage." Fillastre also tells about the Fleece of Gedeon, Jason, Mesa, Job, and David, in a series of uncompleted essays, designed to encompass much of human history.[15]

Does the revival of the myth of Jason within a chivalric Order give rise only to literary works, or is it followed by an actual odyssey? Such, indeed, was the wish of Philip the Good: he expected his knights to be willing to go and fight the Saracens, an expectation clearly written in the statutes of 1430. In 1441, he gave his ducal squire, Geoffroy de Thoisy, the task of preparing and leading a naval expedition to win back "holy Christendom" imperilled by the "sultan of Babylon." A skillful tactician, he managed to prevent enemy attacks on Rhodes. Thus enheartened, the knights of the Golden Fleece wanted to proceed: Jean Germain, Chancellor of the Order, delivered in 1451, at the meeting of the Chapter, a forceful talk advocating a second expedition to support Byzantium. Charles VII did not want to get involved, and what occurred two years later is well known. Nonetheless, in 1454, at the Banquet of the Pheasant given by Philip—where people took the pledge, over a pheasant carried by a 'Golden Fleece' King of Arms, to win back Constantinople—Thoisy and other knights offered their services for another crusade. On this occasion a pantomime in three acts was performed, heralding Raoul Lefèvre's work and the work ascribed to Chastellain. Seven years later, in 1461, when the Chapter of the Golden Fleece met at Saint Omer, Philip, while receiving an embassy from the oriental princes, is reported to have said:

> Lo and behold! The Magi have come from the East, following the star they could see over the West, that is, to you who wear the noble Fleece, and whose power has now spread far and wide, radiating to the shores of the Orient, so much so that it gives light to its princes and nations, and guides them to you, who are the true image of God!

In 1464, Geoffroy de Thoisy, a name which clearly marked him out for Odyssean adventures, was again asked to oversee the preparation in Marseilles of another expedition against the infidels, to which Louis XI, like his predecessor, did not give his support.[16]

Be that as it may, the plan for a crusade against the Saracens was taken over a hundred years later by the fifth and sixth sovereigns of the Order, Charles Quint and Philip II, who also chartered routes to the new world. Finally, it was also at the time of Philip the Good that Henry the Navigator launched his expeditions from Centra, a place taken in 1415 by the troops of John the First. In 1436, Henry's troops pushed as far as the place once reached by Hannon the Phoenician, while his sailors and cartographers discovered and described the shores of the Rio del Ouro.

What were the Portuguese expecting, on the clifftops of Sagres? Not only spices and vanilla, of course, but fabled lands lying beyond the ocean and the skyline, and golden fleeces. To match the Far East there is now a Far West, an Odyssean adventure toward the bed of the sun: two opposite vectors connecting, however, in the North (the summit of the triangle) through Burgundy and its Golden Fleece. (Isabel of Portugal and Burgundy was eventually regarded by some as the very symbol of the Fleece.) But while the troops from Burgundy and Portugal were thus scouring the world, a long-lived tale was taking root, according to which the great wealth of Charles the Bold, son of Philip, came through the Chrysopoeia. And this drew the bonds between the Golden Fleece and alchemy closer.

This trend found further strong support in what is called the euhemerist currents. In the third century, B.C., Euhemerus saw in the

Greek gods actual heroes or colonizers who, according to popular belief, were raised to divinity after their death. Henceforth, "euhemerist" refers to an interpretation of the myths which derives them from history. There is a passage in Pliny's *Natural History* (1.33, c.5) which supports both euhemeristic and esoteric readings of the myth of the Golden Fleece. Pliny writes: "Salauces ruled in Colchis, and Esubopos, of whom it is said he found an as yet unmined soil (*terram virginem*), wherefrom he extracted great amounts of silver and gold, in the land of the Samnites people, famous by the way for their golden skins (*velleribus aureis*)." Later, the expression "*terra virgo*" will sometimes be interpreted as "virginal soil" by the adepts of the hermetic art, although Pliny probably just meant "virgin soil," that is, "a hill not yet opened" by mining. Also, there were some regions in Colchis where river gold was collected by means of skins, whose bristles retained gold particles in suspension.[17]

These historical interpretations have complex and very interesting developments. Thanks to the work of Robert Halleux, it is now possible to unravel their intricacies. Three distinct interpretations may be considered:

a) A technical interpretation: the Golden Fleece was a sieve. The hairs of an animal (a he-goat, a ram) help to collect the particles of gold. This is the view of Plutarch (v.50–125) and, before him, that of Strabon as well (v.58–v.25), who mentioned the use of troughs (for the treatment of alluvia). About the country of the Soanes, in Armenia, Strabon wrote: "It is said that in their country torrents carry away gold, and that the barbarians collect it in mangers pierced with holes and in hairy skins; and this is how the legend of the golden fleece originated." To this reading may be related the mythological interpretation of the birth of the Ram out of the Neptunian ocean.

b) A chrysographic interpretation: the Golden Fleece was a method by means of which one could write on parchments in gold letters. This is the interpretation of Charax of Pergamos, who, around the second or third century A.D., wrote a euhemeristic chronicle in which he interpreted myths historically. It was retained by Eustathios, who quoted this author: "Charax says that the golden fleece is a method for writing in gold (*chrysographia*) on parchment, because of which, according to him, the Argo expedition was launched."

c) An alchemical interpretation: the Golden Fleece was a book of alchemy. Such is the interpretation of John of Antioch (610 A.D.), a Syro-Palestinian author who wrote a chronicle of the world, now lost. He is said to have lived in the reign of Heraclitus (a key period, Robert Halleux notes, for the integration of alchemy in Byzantium). This author wrote: "Jason and his men, crossing the Euxine, arrived in Colchis, took Medea and what was called the golden fleece; which was not, as said poetically, a golden fleece, but a book written on a skin, expounding a way to produce gold chemically."

These interpretations from Strabon, Charax, and John of Antioch were taken up and later copied by some Byzantines. In this way, we find Strabon's interpretation in Eustathios (twelfth century), John of Antioch's in the Suidas (not an actual figure, but an encyclopedia, the *Souda,* late tenth century), and in the pseudo-Eudocia Makremboli-tissa, who mentioned it in her *Violarum* (a mythographic compilation ascribed to her, but which probably developed in the sixteenth century on the basis of the *Souda*). We find Charax' interpretation in Eustathios (cf. *supra*), and therefore in the pseudo-Eudocia. In addition to these interpretations, there are also two traditions. On the one hand, Colchis had an auriferous soil, from which she derived her prosperity; on the other hand, there was in Colchis at least one gold statue, a notion that gained ground through Palaiphatos.[18]

At the same time, in late antiquity a new trend emerged, interpreting mythology in terms of alchemy: that is, a reduction of the stories of the gods to allegories of the processes involved in the Great Work. The best-known reference to this is from Olympiodorus (fifth century A.D.), a Greek alchemist who wrote a book about the divine and sacred art. He tells us that "all the ancients concealed the alchemical art under the multiplicity of discourses." Though he did not mention the Fleece, this reading, in time, became increasingly popular. In a way, his theory is in keeping with John of Antioch's view (chronologically, the latter comes shortly after him). Olympiodorus' text, and those of the above-mentioned Byzantines (tenth, eleventh, and twelfth centuries), make up a collection of interpretations, some of which were frequently pursued.[19] In view of their significance for posterity, let us quote here two of these Byzantines, the Suidas and the pseudo-Eudocia. The Suidas reads:

> It is the Golden Fleece that Jason brought across after he went to Colchis with the Argonauts, sailing through the Black Sea, and after he brought with him also Medea, the daughter of King Aetes. However, it was not a skin as legend would have it, but a book written on skins and teaching how gold could be made chemically, artifically. Which is why the early books have aptly called this writing the golden fleece, because of the art it contained.

The so-called Eudocia Augusta reproduces the accounts of the Suidas and Eustathios in her *Violarium* without identifying them. The passage reads:

Many have said that the ram's skin was in gold, including Appollonios, the author of the Argonautica, while Simonidas held that it was made of purple. Denys of Mitylene declares that there was a man by name of Krios who was Phrixos' preceptor, and that the skin of the golden fleece was not according to its poetical descriptions, but that it was a book written on a skin and expounding a means to make gold alchemically. Therefore, he says, people of these times, quite naturally, would call this skin "the golden skin" in view of what could be achieved through it. And Kharax himself says that the golden fleece is a treatise of chrysography written down on parchments and for which, such was its importance, the fleet of Argos was built.[20]

So, according to these Byzantines, the Golden Fleece was nothing but a parchment, and what the Argonauts pursued in Colchis was none other than a text teaching about the chrysopoeia and written on a ram's skin. This is an interesting interpretation, in line with both the euhemeristic and the mythical trend. On the one hand, it reduces the myth of Jason to so-called historical reality, and at the same time it gives a prominent place to myth, recognizing that an object—a skin bearing a formula or sublime revelations—could have such appeal as to bring about an expedition. Let us refrain, however, from seeing some hermeneutical theory behind this, as in Olympiodorus: the Byzantines are merely giving a few simple hints.

During the Middle Ages Olympiodorus' idea appeared again. It is found particularly in two authors, who, unfortunately, did not mention the Golden Fleece; but what they said about other myths inspired others later on to adopt a similar interpretation. First, Albert the Great (1193-1280), in his *De Mineralibus,* who attempted to reduce some aspects of Greek mythology to processes of operative chemistry; thus, the Gorgon's head, according to him, corresponded to the mineral kingdom. A century later, Petrus Bonus, of Ferrare, offered other mythological scenarios along the same line in his *Pretiosa Margarita novella* (1330), a famous alchemical text, from which many Renaissance authors drew.[21] Finally, it is likely that Philip the Good himself was thinking about alchemy when founding his Order.

ARTISTS, SCHOLARS, AND EARLY HERMENEUTISTS: FROM THE RENAISSANCE TO GUILIELMUS MENNENS

The allegorizing interpretation of the Greek myths was a characteristic feature of the Renaissance; it included the theme, among others, of the Golden Fleece which, as we just saw, had not yet been much elaborated upon. Original exegeses, primarily alchemical, will crop up. This trend was fostered by the growing interest in ancient texts, particularly from the late fifteenth century. Apollonios of Rhodes' (third century B.C.) *Argonautica* appeared in a number of manuscripts, including Laurenzio Alopa's fine incunable, in Florence, published in 1496 and re-edited several times. Valerius Flaccus' exegeses, written in 70 A.D., had about twenty-four editions, from the fifteenth (1474, first edition) to the eighteenth centuries.

Made in the middle or in the second half of the fifteenth century, a series of drawings ascribed to Maso Finiguerra (published by Sidney Colvin in 1898) contains a plate featuring Jason (cf. fig.I), and next to it another one portraying Hermes Trismegistus.[22] Christian and pagan motifs, mixed and infused with hermetics, are also engraved on stone: the castle of Jacques Coeur, in Bourges (first half of the fifteenth century), is a well-known example, but does not contain, it seems, any design directly related to the Golden Fleece. The castle of the Plessis-Bourré (Louis XI's Chancellor of the Exchequer) and built from 1468 to 1473, is more relevant to our purpose: Bourré, whose armorial bearings derive precisely from the ram's skin (cf. fig.III), represents rams fighting. Later we shall see that Eugène Canseliet discussed these symbols.[23]

In Bourges, from 1487 to 1518, a magnificent mansion in the spirit of the Italian Renaissance was built by Jean Lallemant and his son, named after him, who were members of the chivalric Order of Our Lady of the Round Table. This was the Hôtel Lallemant, regarded as one of the great 'philosophers' houses in Europe, and which, for this reason, caught Fulcanelli's attention. Among the numerous motifs directly inspired from the art of Hermes, let us mention the one concerning the Golden Fleece: on the Chapel's bas-relief (cf. fig.IV), a stone-engraved landscape set off with colors (in the manner of the loggia's Saint Christopher in the same mansion) features a forest of oaks (with which Argo was built) with large boulders. On one of them, to the right, lies the ram's skin watched by a frightening dragon in profile. Perhaps Jason was also here, at the foot of an oak tree, but he has been worn away over the course of time. The scene is filled with other creatures of uncertain identities.[24]

These are certainly not the only traces of the myth on Renaissance stone. We should also remember an author frequently quoted by several alchemists in connection with the Golden Fleece: Aloisius Marlianus who, in 1517, before the Chapter of the Order of that name, delivered an address in which he told of the ship Argo and the members of its crew. However, alchemical exegeses had actually started two years before, in 1515, in Venice, with the publication of the *Chrysopoeia,* by the great poet Giovanni Aurelio Augurelli (1454–cir. 1537) who, after dedicating to Pope Leon X, in 1514, this splendid hermetic poem in Latin hexameters, produced another shorter one entitled *Vellus Aureum.* The Pope is said to have rewarded the author with an empty purse, on the grounds that this is all an alchemist needs, since he has already more than enough to fill it up![25]

Implicit in the text itself, the hermeticizing allegory appears explicitly in the title, as well as in the conclusion: "And returning to my fatherland as a Jason, / I brought across the Golden Fleece from the blessed country of Colchis" (*in patriam rediens, sic alter Jason, / Aurea foelici devexi vellera Colcho*). With this poem the initial impetus was given. An alchemical ship, with the Golden Fleece as its figurehead, sailed out of Venice on a beautiful hermeneutical odyssey. Henceforth, an interesting collection of writings developed, devoted to the alchemical interpretation of Greek mythology; however, the Golden Fleece was not always in evidence. And in the realm of iconography, the fact that there are vessels lying at anchor alongside alchemical landscapes which adorn lavishly illustrated books, does not mean for sure that this is the fleet of Argo. Yet, at times, we might be tempted to believe that it is so; for instance, when looking at the illustrations of the 1526 *De Alchemia.*[26] But there is no Golden Fleece, even implicitly, in Giovanni Bracesco da Iorci Novi's frequently copied Italian dialogues (*La espositione di Geber* and *Il Legno della vita,* 1542.[27] Bracesco wants to show, for instance, how behind the name and fable of Demogorgon lies the matter of alchemical art, or how the story of Daedalus and Icarus refers to putrefaction and distillation;[28] a method which had quickly gained ground and was applied before long to our ram.

The first to do this with accuracy and with a wealth of detail seems to be Gianfrancesco Pico della Mirandola (cir. 1469–1533) in his *De Auro,*[29] which was written just after the sack of Rome in 1527, but not published until after 1586. Pico, a nephew of the illustrious author of the *Conclusiones* and the *Oratio Hominis Dignitate,* knew what he was talking about as he himself practiced alchemy. The famous mythographer Lilio Gregorio Giraldi, whose odd drawings illustrated ancient mythology,[30] has left us a valuable account of a conversation he had with him.[31] He manages to extricate himself, although ruined, from the Roman disaster, and comes for refuge to La Mirandola where he finds Pico at his furnaces. He does not come empty-handed, for he brings to his friend an alchemical manuscript by Michael Psellos. Forgetting for a moment political upheavals, the two men try to draw the secrets of the art from the myth of Hercules' golden apples and the myth of Jason. To this end, they scrutinize both Psellos' manuscript and Apollonios of Rhodes' *Argonautica*. What does Apollonios mean when he writes that the Fleece turned into gold at Mercury's mere touch?[32] How much of that story is real? Both adepts also discuss some of the above-mentioned texts which, as Renaissance scholars, they know quite well. They discuss the tradition that the shepherds of Colchis became rich by selling the wool of their sheep; about the auriferous rivers flowing in this country, from which gold was collected by means of skins used as sieves, according to Eustathios' and Strabon's accounts; about other writers for whom the image of the golden-haired sheep arose because the barbarians of this region were simultaneously rich and poor; finally, about the interpretation that the Fleece was a parchment bearing a text that contained the secrets of the chrysopoeia, an interpretation the two men found in the Suidas.

In *De Auro*, Pico mainly relates these conversations with Giraldi, quoting ancient writers such as Varron, Strabon, Suidas, Psellos, and the Orphic verses devoted to this fable.[33] But he also seeks to derive its alchemical meaning. The book containing the secrets of the art was actually written on a ram's skin[34] and kept in the house of King Aëtes. The names "Dragon" and "Mercury" refer to processes: gold is obtained through the touch of Mercury, and the ever-watchful Dragon mounts guard over Phrixos' fleece. Under the tree where this fleece was hanging, there was a field with a few items used for fixing quicksilver: small trees and vegetables, and also the chrysanthemum, that is, vitriol.[35] The main characteristic of this reflection, as expressed both in Pico's dialogues with Giraldi and in the *De Auro* by the same Pico, is that the euhemerist interpretation goes along with the belief in the reality of transmutation, and thus unfolds from both history and myth. Such a paradoxical reading reveals a synthetic, non-exclusive approach. It seems that for Pico and Giraldi the validity of historical, geographical, and economical readings does not exclude a material and spiritual alchemy behind the veil of real happenings.

Another mythologist, Noël Conti, as celebrated as Giraldi, listed some of the material related to Jason's adventures in his 1551 *Mythologiae*.[36] Next came the publication of a work by the paracelsian Jacques Gohory (1520–1576), its Latin and French translation respectively entitled *Hystoria Jasonis* and *Livre de la conqueste de la toison d'or* (1563). This is a short text—only four pages—but it is adorned with twenty-six plates representing the hero's odyssey.[37] One continues on the path paved by Augurelli who, poetically, had identified the expres-

sion "Golden Fleece" with "hermetic art." *Chrysorrhoas* (1561) opens
with a dialogue about skin parchments and Medea's skills at restoring
AEson to youth, the author advising a careful reading of Apollonius of
Rhodes' many pages where metals are mentioned.[38] The century ended
with the publication, in 1598, of a collection of texts that was to become
famous, and was reedited several times: *Aureum Vellus oder Guldin
Schatz- und Kunstkammer,*[39] in which the Golden Fleece is mentioned
only in the title.[40] First, this book finally established *"aureum vellus"* as
a synonym for "chrysopoeia" or "alchemy"; second, it ushered in a
"germanization" of the Golden Fleece, in that the Fleece then made its
way into the hermetic literature of the German countries. It was also
one of the first vernacular alchemical compilations. The editor associated the name of Salomon Trismosin with that of Paracelsus and the
ram's skin.

With the seventeenth century, alchemical literature and iconography reached their heights; but it seems that only in the first third of
the century did the tale of the golden ram receive a hermetic-inspired
interpretation. We find this in the work of two alchemists: one, Mennens,
was rather obscure, while the other was the best-known alchemist of
the time, Michael Maier. From the artistic point of view, Johann Valentin
Andreae's novel, published in 1616, also gave a prominent place to this
myth. Like most authors interested in this myth, these three were
German.

In 1604, in Antwerp, a large and fine work was published in Latin. It
has unjustly fallen into oblivion, although it was reprinted in the
Theatrum Chemicum, that great alchemical summa of the seventeenth
century. Its title is *Aurei Velleris sive sacrae Philosophiae Vatum
selectae unicae mysteriorumque ac Dei, Naturae et Artis admirabilium, libri tres.* The author, Guilielmus Mennens (1525–1608), was
also well-versed in poetry, natural history, theology, and medicine; he
was the editor of Adrianus Scorelius' poems.[41] After G. Pico della
Mirandola, he is the second author who paid such attention to the
golden ram. Of this large theosophical book, which deserves to be translated and reprinted, it is true that only a few pages are devoted to this
theme. But they are interesting and inspired. Mennens does not limit
himself to a description of Colchis' auriferous rivers, or to the tradition
that Philip of Burgundy had a treasure produced by the chrysopoeia
and comparable to that of Solomon.[42] He also offers an alchemical and
moral exegesis of the tale. Let us note some of the correspondences he
established.

The Hebrews possessed the secrets of the chrysopoeia: coming out
of Egypt, Moses ordered them to take along the golden and silver vessels,

that is, the secret treasures collected by the people of Israel by means of the art, of which Egypt is the motherland. After he won his battle in Egypt against Achilles, who had himself proclaimed emperor in Alexandria, Diocletian had all the books on alchemical art searched out and burnt, so that his enemies, once they had rallied, could not make use of them against the Romans.[43] What they contained could be used not only to secure material goods, but they could also be interpreted on two other levels: medicine (that is, health) and divine philosophy. Etymology gives us a clue about the 'medical' aspect of the myth of Jason. Medea is the symbol par excellence of the art of healing through the knowledge of metals, as of course, the role she plays in this story clearly shows. But what is more, her name can be related to *"medela"* (medicine, remedy), or to *"medeor, mederi"* (to medicate); and the name Jason also derives from a Greek word with the same meaning.[44] Interpreting the whole myth as material, therapeutic, and spiritual alchemy, Mennens embraced the view that the book, a treasury of wisdom, was a skin; which interpretation he felt gave it a 'hieroglyphic' aspect allowing for a hermeneutics that goes beyond the material level. He believed this text was engraved in golden letters, whose meaning cannot be grasped at once, a hidden meaning, as befits an art leading ultimately to a divine philosophy. Poets used to conceal the mysteries of natural and sacred things behind the fable; it was all the easier for the image of a golden fleece to take hold since auriferous rivers flow from springs in the foothills of the Caucasus, and their gold, mingled with dust, is collected in skins dipped into this water by the local people.[45]

The divine philosophy taught under the veil of myth is designed for those able to understand the symbolic meaning of the ship of 'gymnasium' Argo, for we find here heroes, divine and outstanding figures, masters (*proceres*), exposed to many storms upon the ocean and to hazardous situations. But they manage to overcome all these ordeals. In the same way, those who understand the message will learn how to rise above the multiplicity of human opinion, how to go beyond the thorns and monsters they represent. At last, they will be able to reach the peaceful roads, the longed-for haven, the isle of Colchis where the Ram grazes. They will find Medea, a symbol for a perfect knowledge of things natural and divine. As to the sleeping, conquered dragon watching over, or rather obscuring from view, the Golden Fleece, Mennens says he should be looked on as gross ignorance of the principles he reminds us about in his theosophical book, and ignorance wrapped in myriads of far-fetched opinions.

More alchemically, Mennens sees the hermetic vessel in the steel plough to which Jason must yoke the two bulls. In these creatures vomiting fire, he perceives the matter that has to be thrown into the vessel at the right time. The four-acre field of Mars stands for the four elements. Hermes Trismegistus says: "The sun is its father, the moon is its mother, and the wind has borne it in its womb, its nurse is the earth." As a matter of fact, he who knows not of these things cannot proceed toward the Work; everything will turn against him; he will experience nothing but misery and sorrow. For indeed, what emerges initially from this matter is white spirits, so called because of the dragon's white teeth. According to the fable of Jason, these teeth, when falling on the ground, turned into dreadful fighters. However, Jason was able to conquer them with his spear. Similarly, the philosophers' fire has the power to destroy the white spirits, if one knows how to throw the stone in their midst and tightly shut the vessel so they cannot fly away. When all the dragons have been conquered through that singular procedure, the adept will receive the riches of the Golden Fleece. It is enough, Mennens says, to have expounded to the studious seeker these few elements of the hermetic Arcanes![46]

Our myth, in this book, seems an occasion for a number of cosmogonic and cosmosophic speculations, most of which have absolutely no relevance to it. It is used as a starting point for bold reflection or as a support for meditation. And yet the theme of the light, touched upon here, is indeed linked to the gold of the Ram. Painters, says Mennens, can best reproduce a flame when using shining thin flakes of gold. Thus, from the prototype of the Golden Fleece, bright flames shoot up all about.[47] Mennens also devotes two substantial pages to the symbol of the Ram itself, essential, he says rightly, for understanding the myth which gave rise to his book. One tradition would derive "Aries" from *"aris,"* that is, "altars" (*ara, arae*) because, of all animals, from the beginning of the world, he was destined to altars—in other words to immolation— as a pure, excellent, and innocent sacrifice to God, the Creator of all things. The Passover is observed in March, a Ram month. Others derive "Aries" from *"arètè,"* that is, "virtue, courage" (*virtus*). The ram is sacred to Mars because he is brave, a leader of herds; he inspires respect—at his mere sight even elephants run away. Mennens also stresses the meaning of the Ram in the zodiac. Among other traditions, he notices that if, in the sky, the Lion gives way to the Ram, it shows that force and tyranny give way to indulgence, matter to form, dispute to peace, eternal darkness to light. Porta claims that people who have been through many dangers sleep in ram's skins. Apollo, who is said to have discovered harmonic chords, played an instrument whose strings were made of ram's nerves. Just as the sun is always shining, so this animal can see at night as well as in the daytime; in fact, his liver is said to cure eye diseases. Finally, let us mention how Mennens, after this digression, returns to alchemy. Since all metals are partly made of fire, they are ruled by Mars, whose house is the Ram (goods, riches, symbolized by gold); so it is no wonder that the Romans honored Jupiter Ammonius, Mammon, at Mount Aventin, in the form of a ram, an idol most vital to Egypt, the land of gold, silver, and alchemy![48]

THE GOLDEN FLEECE AS A SIGN OF THE LABORATORY: MICHAEL MAIER, J. V. ANDREAE, AND SEVENTEENTH CENTURY ALCHEMY

Drawn at the time of the publication of Mennens's book, the awkward, but suggestive illustrations of the *Speculum Veritatis* (the manuscript is in the Vatican) appeared as secrets of the Great Work, more or less visible behind the veil of mythological symbology. The first in this series shows a ram looking like Jason's; thus is the 'laboratory'—represented by the whole set of pictures—somehow presided over and prefigured by the Golden Fleece (cf. fig.VI).

Michael Maier's very first book, *Arcana Arcanissima, hoc est Hieroglyphica Graeca,* published in Oppenheim around 1610,[49] devotes about fifteen pages to the Fleece. Although his work is not nearly as wide in scope as Mennens' treatment of the subject, Pernety later drew from *Arcana* in his treatise on ancient fables, a work that has achieved a high measure of success. After mentioning some of the rather historicizing interpretations listed above, Maier declares that the Fleece of Phrixos and Jason should be understood above all as a supreme medicine for the human body, even more than as the symbol of the chrysopoeia. As a matter of fact, true medicine is concerned less with caring for metals than for living bodies. Based on these considerations, there evolves a theory of colors and some arithmological reflections. At first the Fleece was probably white, and then turned red when gilded over by Mercury (see *Georgica,* 21). In these two colors lies the principle of the art. Maier points out the medical meaning of the name Medea: "she who restores to youth" AEson, Jason's father, and then Jason himself. The discussion on numbers concerned the time spent by the Argonauts on their voyage which, according to the author, could not have exceeded twelve months.

At least two of Maier's other works deal with the Fleece. What remains of his most famous work, *Atalanta Fugiens,* was published in 1617.[50] This is a series of fifty emblematic plates, each with a commentary and a musical score in the form of a fugue. Emblem 49 features the myth of Orion (cf. fig.VII). In order to give Hyrieus a son, Vulcan, Phoebus, and Hermes threw their semen, or rather their sacred urine, into an oxskin where it remained for ten months; out of this Orion was born (cf. Ovid, *Fasti,* 395 ff.). The picture represents these four charac- ters, three of them holding the ox skin. The caption looks like an al- chemical interpretation: "Of three fathers the child of wisdom is born; / The sun is the first, and Vulcan the second; / the man adept in his art is the third father."[51] Just as the seed germinated in the ox skin, Maier explains in his commentary, so were Achilles, Jason, and Hercules turned over to Chiron to receive his teaching—that is, for their minds to expand. During the birth of Orion, Mercury provided the matter, Apollo the form, and Vulcan the heat or external efficient cause. Admittedly, here it is an ox skin, not a ram's skin; however, as is clearly suggested by the commentary,[52] Maier meant to deal with both myths at the same time. As a matter of fact, in the commentary on emblem 44, he places Jason among the mythological figures symbolizing 'the artist', that is, the alchemist: Hercules, Ulysses, Theseus, Pirithous.

Finally, for the third time, Maier includes in one of his works, *Sym- bola Aureae Mensae,*[53] a reflection on the Golden Fleece. The chapter devoted to the 'chemical colonies of the Egyptians' begins with the story of Cadmus and Agenor, and tells about Colchis:

> Ammianus I.22 says of the people of Colchis that they are the first descendants of the Egyptians. Diodorus calls them "Egyptian colonists living in the Pount," because of the mines. The allegory of the Golden Fleece is attributed to the people of Colchis because this country was rich in metals and in the minerals needed for the alchemical art. In the sacred wood of Mars, the son of the Sun revealed to several artisans the sheep skin gilded by Mercury. Jason (that is, the physician of astute strategies) finally got hold of it through the expert guidance of Medea (that is, Theoretical Reason). First, the dragon has to be robbed of his teeth (which are the purified matter of the art) with the help of a narcotic made from an herb collected when the sun enters Capricorn, for at this time its roots are more potent. Second, the teeth have to be sowed into a suitable soil cared for by a water-bearing gardener (that is, it must be damp or profusely watered). Third, the soil must be ploughed by bulls and sowed with the seed. Then, from every- where, arise fierce cries of men who grow bigger and bigger, and start killing one another. This is when the goal is achieved—obtain- ing the golden stone.[54]

Furthermore, Maier has a fictitious character visit the four continents. They are each presided over by one element: Europe by earth, America by water, Asia by air, and Africa by fire. After leaving America, this character travels through vast stretches of land, until he reaches Asia, which should be understood as the Middle East and Near East, where Jason once went for the Fleece. As a matter of geographical fact, Colchis belongs to that area. Almost the entire passage on this continent is devoted to Jason. One day, this character goes to the sacred wood of Mars and King AEtes, son of the Sun. There he meets an old man of imposing appearance and noble face who greets him. He asks the old man about Jason. The old man tells him he is Jason himself. As he sees the traveler shudder, not surprisingly, Medea's consort tells him he has nothing to fear, and says he has been living here since ancient times. Jason also says that he is willing to tell his story, provided the traveler focuses on its meaning rather than on the words. Then he proceeds to tell about the stratagems of Medea, who put a narcotic down the dragon's throat, and who poured clear water to extinguish the flames shooting forth from the oxen's mouth. Unexpectedly, he adds that Medea had agreed to give him "the images of the Sun and the Moon, without which I would not get anywhere." Now it is up to the traveler to look for Medea, who is still alive, somewhere in that region of Asia called Media. Pondering over these words, the traveler finally understands them as containing the secret of the 'medicine' that he was looking for and that Phoenix—the founder of Phoenicia, Cadmus' brother and Agenor's son—also wanted to discover, a medicine symbolized by the Golden Fleece, "for the hair of the golden creature and the feathers of the Phoenix bird both relate to the same thing."[54] (cf. *infra,* Appendix 1, # 2).

In the finest alchemical story of modern times, *Chymische Hochzeit Christiani Rosencreutz* (1616),[56] we see how the hero is admitted, on the third of seven 'days', into the Order of the Golden Fleece with a winged lion: "Before we take our seats, there come two page boys who hand to each of us, on behalf of the bridegroom, the golden fleece, with a winged lion, requesting that we wear it at table and behave with due respect to the reputation and greatness of an Order into which our admission will shortly be confirmed by His Majesty with pomp and circumstance."[57] Associating the lion and the ram is part of a traditional symbology. Besides Mennens' above-mentioned references on astrology, this is also suggestive of the fixed and coagulating principle, or Sulphur, commonly represented by the lion, and which therefore is naturally associated with the volatile, aerial (mercurial) nature of the ram. This association is further stressed by the fact that the lady, like Christian, is wearing the golden fleece and the lion, whence he infers that she might be the president of the Order.[58] On the fourth day, he is given a new fleece adorned with gems (cf. the original, *infra,* Appendix 1, # 4):

> After we had washed at the fountain and taken a sip out of a golden cup, we had to go back to the hall with the lady, in order to put on new clothes, garments embroidered with gold and adorned with magnificent flowers. Each of us was also presented with a new golden fleece spangled with precious stones, their many virtues coming from the powers radiating from each of them. Its pendant was a heavy gold plate, with the sun and the moon on one side and this maxim on the other side: The moon will shine as brightly as the sun, and the sun will be sevenfold brighter than now.[59]

In a seminal work devoted to Johann Valentin Andreae, Roland Edighoffer compares Medea, who may symbolize the dark forces of Nature, to the sleeping Venus whom Christian beholds in the subterranean halls of the castle: approaching her is indeed unsafe. Power and volatility combine in the sign of the winged lion who, in the *Chemical Marriage,* is a companion to the Golden Fleece. Above all, for Christian Rosencreuz, the gold of the Fleece was somehow the sign of a promise, an invitation to a spiritual journey. But this hero was to receive something more: the Order of the Golden Stone, a kind of supreme consecration. At the end of the novel he then gives away his Golden Fleece as a token of humility, a humility which, according to Roland Edighoffer, would mean that he gives up an initiatory rite. This would suggest that he substitutes the *Agnus Dei* for the hermetic ram: "We gave thanks to God, and in His honor I gave away my Golden Fleece and my hat, leaving them here as a sign of eternal remembrance."[60]

While Maier favors the medical interpretation of this symbology, other writers of the time offer an ever-growing number of mythological appellations referring to recipes. Thus we find such names as "Mitigated Dragon," "Imperial Eagle,"—and "Golden Fleece." For instance, we learn that to 'prepare' the latter, one must first of all collect the dew of May in a wheat field, preferably before sunrise when the weather is fine. Jean Béguin's *Tyrocinium Chymicum* (Cologne, 1611), which has been translated several times, reflects this tendency.[61] During the seventeenth century a number of books associate, in their title or contents, the Golden Fleece with alchemy, but usually do not go beyond mere allusion. The Golden Fleece was referred to as a mere substitute for the philosophers' stone or the Great Work. I will list here the chronology of those that have come to my attention. First, we have the fine *Toyson d'Or ou la Fleur des Thrésors,* published in 1612 (and probably as early as 1602) by Charles Sevestre, in Paris.[62] Its title page gives the exact counterpart of the 1598 German book's title (the author, whether real or fictitious, is said, as in 1598, to be Solomon Trismosin). This French print is but a free translation, signed L.I., of only one of the German treatises, *Splendor Solis,* a translation dedicated to François de Bourbon. In his lengthy dedication, L.I. compares his own alchemical journey to an odyssean voyage: he has "infused the ship with a great science, to cruise along the shores of his vast universe and gather from the flowers of the best Philosophers a hive of sweet honey." L.I. lays the "fresh fruit" of his "Hermes tree" at the feet of François de Bourbon.[63]

Then there are books in which the Golden Fleece appears mostly on the title page, or as a short metaphorical reference in the text itself. Andreas Libavius, a noted professor of history and poetry in Iena, a supporter of alchemy who fought Eraste and Riolan, tells of the Fleece in the first of the two volumes of his *Commentarium Alchymiae,* published in Frankfurt in 1606.[64] Johann Siebmacher's *Das Güldene Vliess,* written in 1607, was published in 1609 and had four subsequent editions. There is no mention of the Fleece in the text, but it appears in a fine illustration in the 1736 edition.[65]

The appetite for allegorical interpretations of mythology was whetted once again by Clovis Hesteau de Nuysement's *Traittez du vray sel,*[65] inspired by Bracesco. The passage concerning our myth gives only a poor idea of the inspired poetry and theosophy pervading this work; all the same, it is welcome and stands as a model of the genre. For this reason it is quoted in full (cf. *infra,* Appendix 1, # 3). Telling us about the origin of the "secret poetic fictions," most of them "invented only to hint at the admirable operations of natural spagyric," Hesteau goes on to say that it is the same with the 'fiction' of Jason. The latter is so interesting that the writer agrees to depart from alchemical secrecy and give us some clues. Thus "Medea" means "cogitation, meditation, or investigation," and derives from a word meaning "principle, origin, source, or reason." To Jason, a seeker and a philosopher, she taught two things: the transformation of metals and a rejuvenating medicine. This was teaching which bore fruit, notwithstanding "a long and laborious navigation, followed by endless perilous hazards," for seeking truth and experiencing life do not always take us safe into port "of this vast sea of Nature." Then, without any transition, he leads us into the alchemical interpretation of the myth. The bulls to be tamed are the furnaces. Their fire-spitting eyes and throats symbolize the openings of the athanor, designed as heat regulators during the operation. The dragon represents the mercury to be fixed. The field of Mars, out of which fully equipped soldiers spring up, is the alchemical vessel made, according to Nuysement, "of good terracotta, and not of iron or glass." After Jason had performed his feat, the dragon still had to be narcotized, so its mouth would stop belching fire and smoke—an activity which, at the operative level, represents the new dissolution and the new fixation. Finally, and more cryptically, he informs us that Jason restores old AEson to youth through "the fermentation and conjunction of the sun butter with the paste of this prepared mercury." Here it is to be noted that symbolism is only marginal. These are only word-to-word correspondences. Pernety's work is no better. Moreover the latter is almost completely lacking in the spiritual flights, in the symbolic interplay of words which pervades other passages of Nuysement's *Traittez.*

There are further interesting, though shorter, references to the Golden Fleece. First, shortly after this *Traittez,* in Großschedel, in 1429;[67] next, in the middle and second half of the century. There is a discussion between two rival scholars, Conring and Borrichius, over the antiquity of the hermetic art and the 'science' of the Egyptians. Hermann Conring, a professor at Helmstadt, a celebrated polygraph opposing the paracelsism of his colleague Borrichius, refers to Jason in *De Hermetica AEgyptiorum vetere et nova Paracelsicorum Medicina,* in 1648.[68] Olaus Borrichius, a professor of botany and chemistry in Copenhagen, did the same in *Hermetis, Aegyptiorum et Chemicorum Sapientia* (1674), and *De Ortu et Progressu Chemiae* (1668), a text popularized by Manget's edition: it is placed at the very beginning of the first volume.[69] Also noteworthy is Johann Ludwig Möglin's alchemical book, published in 1665, where the Golden Fleece appears only on the title page.[70]

We find a little more substance in the strange work published in Ulm in 1680 under the beautiful pseudonym of Johannes De Monte Hermetis. Its title is no less poetic: *Explicatio Centri in Trigono Centri per Somnium. Das ist: Erlaüterung dess Hermetischen Güldenen Fluss.*[71] Although there is no lack of publishers nowadays willing to reprint or even translate ancient books of alchemy, they usually remain on well-trodden paths; but here is a text well worth publishing. Until it is revived in full, let us give the beginning of the address to the reader (cf. the original, *infra,* Appendix 1, # 5):

> You must have heard of the story of that ancient pagan and chivalrous hero, Jason, who, urged by his brave heart, wanted to obtain that which, in his own days, nobody could obtain—namely, the Golden Fleece, of great value and great fame in Greece, which was in a very remote island. He was able to get hold of it, by pro-

pitiating his gods and following the right course of action; also by taking advice from clever people living on that island. He took away the fabulous treasure of that Golden Fleece in a heroic way, and after much effort and labor. I am very well aware that even today there would be such chivalrous heroes willing to fight for the hermetic Golden Fleece, if only they were given some support to this end. That is why I wanted to recall this oft-quoted verse: *Scire tuum nihil est, nisi te scire hoc sciat alter.*[72]

The following year, 1681, saw the publication of Th. Corneille's and Donneau de Visé's play entitled *La Pierre Philosophale,* which must have given people some insight into a group of alchemists belonging to the circle of Louis de Vanens, who was on friendly terms with la Voisin and who was arrested on December 5, 1677. That alchemy could become the subject of a play implies it was both popular and fashionable. This is illustrated in the December 1679 issue of the *Mercure Galant:* here we find a picture representing Jason about to kill with his sword a bull sending out flame and smoke through his nostrils. The caption reads: "Iason puzzle," and the text gives the reader a clue to the puzzle. The *Mercure Galant* publishes the answer in its January 1680 issue:

> The pictorial puzzle was the philosophers' stone. Jason stands for the chemist seeking that stone by blowing into the furnace symbolized by the monster he fights. The bull sends out flames through his nostrils, just as a burning furnace does through its openings. The Golden Fleece hanging to a tree in the print is none other than the philosophers' stone, which the chemist seeks to obtain by trying to find out how to make gold. Such is the explanation given to this puzzle by Mr. Gardien, of Boissimon, Mr. C. D. Minot, of Dijon, and the unknown person of Meaux. Some others thought it was the bomb, or the flintstone, and the gun.[73]

It was in Groningen, shortly after, that Barent Coenders Van Helpen's *L'Escalier des Sages, Ou Trésor de la Philosophie* was published (1686; second edition, in Cologne, 1693), a work with copper plate engravings, thirteen of them borrowing their subject from mythology. One of them, devoted to fire, features a warrior giving a sheep to Hades who carries a funeral torch (cf. figure IX). One may ask oneself, with Jacques Van Lennep, whether or not this could be Jason offering the Golden Fleece he just conquered for Pelias. The ship lying at anchor nearby, in the background, might well be Argo.[74]

As a matter of fact, while the alchemists of the baroque era were inclined to speak about the ram and his gold in terms of a spiritual goal to be reached, this aspect was not accepted by all currents of thought. Thus, in *Frühlingslust,* the mystic Katharina Regina von Greiffenberg tells in verse about golden stars upon the earth, stars moving over trees, shadows filling the space, silvery clouds tinged with sapphire, bushes and forests echoing with musical sounds and arrayed in smaragdine ornaments—a complete setting, the elements of which can be found in any inspired alchemical text—and yet she adds: "Colchis may as well keep its golden skin and his Golden Fleece."[75]

Before leaving the late seventeenth century, let us once again turn toward inscriptions on stones. Built in this period on the Esquilin, the villa of the Marquis Maximilian Palombara was presumably a most wonderful house. Nothing of it remains but some sketches and the frame of a marble door preserved at the Piazza Vittorio Emanuele in Rome. On an outside wall was an inscription saying that inside the compound a palisade contained the Fleece: "ubi vallus claudit vellus." In the entrance hall could be seen, engraved on a slab by Palombara, the following words: "Villae Januam / Tranando / Recludens Jason / Obtinat locuples / Vellus Medae" (Walking through the gate of the villa, Jason discovers and conquers Medea's precious Fleece.) The acrostic "vitriolum" should be noted (this word is a common feature in alchemy). The inscription is dated 1680. In a manuscript in the Vatican Library, the *Ludus Hermeticus,* Palombara writes: "Jasonem unicum / Tu vide strenue / Mare neptunicum" (See how the extraordinary Jason cheerfully and cleverly roams the sea of Neptune). On the Horizontal upper part of the marble door, below Hebrew letters, we read: "Horti magici ingressum Hesperius custodit draco et / sine Alcide Colchias delicias non gustasset Iason" (The dragon of the Hesperides watches over the entrance of the magic garden, and but for Hercules, Jason would not have tasted the delights of Colchis). The gardens of the Palombara villa spreading beyond the gate are thus assimilated to the Hesperides. Above all, mentioning the figure of Jason at this point is a hint (as Mino Gabriele points out) of the soul's journey through the thresholds of initiation, a journey during which the soul puts on a skin, the "skin of the King," spangled with gold or containing sparkles of gold—to which Palombara's book itself means to attest, bearing the title *La Bugia* (1656).[76]

2

From the Age of Enlightenment to Contemporary Hermeneutics

THE ROCOCO COMPASS AND CONCORDANCE: EHRD OF NAXAGORAS

At the dawn of the eighteenth century, there are two noteworthy essays among the series of hermetical writings dealing with the myth of Jason. These are by Johann Ludwig Hannemann, professor of physics in Kiel, whose partially unpublished works amount to one hundred or so, and include several treatises of alchemy:[77] *Xtus in hortum Hesperidum i.e. Parasceve ad aureum vellus,* in 1715,[78] and *Jason, seu Catalogus Testimoniorum Veritatis,* in 1709, both published in Kiel.[79] *Jason* is an interesting collection of ancient and modern alchemical sources; in the preface, the author says he has been studying and supporting natural philosophy for thirty-four years; however, of the many references used to make a case for the reality of transmutation, only one is about the Golden Fleece and it appears in the title. The year 1736 saw the publication of a new edition of Johann Siebmacher's *Das Güldene Vliesse,*[80] adorned with a fine engraving on the title page (cf. figure X) representing the collar of the Order of the Golden Fleece associated with planetary designs and a five-pointed star.

　　Johann Konrad Creiling, professor of mathematics and physics in Tübingen, is said to have been a tower of knowledge and a keen operative. He wrote at least two alchemical works: *Die Edelgeborene Jungfer Alchymia,*[81] in 1730, and *Dissertatio Academica de Auro Vellere aut Possibilitate Transmutationis Metallorum,* in 1737, reedited several times.[82] In this *Dissertatio,* quoting Plutarch, he unhesitatingly adopted the interpretation offered by the Suidas.[83] As the fable clearly shows, he comments, the hazards and difficulties connected with the work cannot be overcome; the coveted pathway is kept closed by the supreme Commander, if the operator does not carry out his work with Medea—that is, Wisdom, the Mistress of all the arts.[84] Speaking of Philip the Good, he remarks that his Order was founded with the emergence in Germany of a number of remarkable inventions, notably printing. Among the attributes of the knights, he stresses the golden chain with its flintstones, and the mottos *"ante ferit quam flamma micat"* and *"pretium non vile laborum."* These mottos, say Creiling, aroused in him a philosophical gusto which prompted him to write his *Dissertatio,* trying thereby to kindle the flames that would illuminate the Golden Fleece, a story which teaches how metals can be transmuted or improved.[85]

But the Enlightenment saw the publication of three works more concerned with the Golden Fleece, and more ambitious in purpose, each from an adept in the hermetic art: Ehrd of Naxagoras, Hermann Fictuld, and Joseph Antoine Pernety. Although Naxagoras' large volume *Aureum Vellus oder Güldenes Vliess* does not deal exclusively with this myth, it gives it a prominent place in many chapters. We still don't know who is hiding behind this pseudonym—maybe one Johann Erhard Neidhold, or Neithold. He does not tell much about himself, except that he has been confined to a Turkish jail in Lischna, Bosnia.[86] Among several other alchemical treatises, he wrote *Alchymia denudata* (1708), and *Chymischer oder Alchimisticher Particular-Zeiger* (1706) which, judging by their various editions, must have met with a certain measure of success. The same is true of his *Aurem Vellus,* first published in 1715 in Giessen, and dedicated to Emperor Charles VI. The second edition, with its long and slightly altered title, (also used in the third edition) was published in Frankfurt in 1731; two years later it was reprinted here with a 62-page supplement entirely devoted to the *Emerald Tablet.*[87] The title explicitly states that the reader will find numerous reflections on our myth: *Aureum Vellus, or Golden Fleece: a Treatise telling about the basis and origin of the very ancient Golden Fleece, what it was in the past, the long and hazardous journey made for its sake, and about those who made it; and finally about how and through whom it became a most respected chivalric Order, why and because of whom this Order is to be preferred to all others, in view of its ancient basis, with no claim to make it a law, so that this Fleece be once again the Fleece of a most noble Order.*[88]

Our author is prolix, no doubt. But the flow of his rather clumsy and at best rococo eloquence carries with it alluvium that we enjoy identifying and sorting out. Here we bathe in warm streams contrasting with the cold compilations cropping up in this late germanic period of humanism. Scholarship and ideas are less subordinated to authorities, to the ancients—although he quotes them profusely—than in most of the hermeneutists of his day and their immediate predecessors. Quite often, his meandering but nevertheless focused eclecticism happily provides for an inspired hermeneutics. He is not the only one to do so: Fictuld could be similarly praised, despite his occasional lack of refinement.

Let us not pay undue attention to the inevitable euhemeristic reminiscences to which others, well before him, so persistently returned. We find them here again, as befits a compiler bound to display knowledge that has become a criterion of credibility. Naxagoras' boldness lay elsewhere. He had equal fascination for two myths that are the expression of the same *topos:* the Golden Fleece and the Emerald Tablet. He deals with both in his book, confidently and ably, and I shall return to his treatment of the Tablet in another study devoted to that subject. The accounts of the myth of Jason are discussed extensively, after the reader has been informed that the Golden Fleece of mythology and the burgundian Order of that name are two different things. Naxagoras wanted to reassure the Order's dignitaries: never will it be stated that this knighthood was based on securing the alchemical gold, or that it was founded by Jason himself. We might, he says, differentiate between "Knight of the Golden Fleece" and "Knight of the Golden Stream"—playing upon the words *"Vliess"* and *"Fluss."* But, he wrote later on, the Order founded by Philip the Good may be taken as a model by any true chivalry, that of the Golden Stream, as he called it. This is an ideal that would have inspired the ancient, or mythical, Knights of the Sun, of whom there is no record in history and who, according to Naxagoras, were close to the ideal of the Brothers of the Rosy Cross.[89]

The book consists of ten chapters, the first three being devoted to Jason: his story according to mythology; the nature of the ram and his fleece according to ancient records; the reasons that prompted philosophers and poets to describe the hermetic art in the form of parables and allegories, notably in the fable of Jason, and how they could do it.[90] Chapter IX deals more particularly with the *Emerald Tablet,*[91] along with the *Supplementum* in the 1733 edition. The other chapters are devoted to alchemy and its history.

Recalling the interpretation that has come down from Strabon, Plutarch, and Eustathios, Naxagoras ventures to say that a royal prince such as Jason would not have considered setting off on such a costly expedition for the sake of a skin that any of his emissaries could have brought back to him.[92] He censures Johann Gerlach Wilhelm, who thought the myth originated from an expedition planned by bandits (living in the country later known as the Netherlands) who went to steal gold in Mingrelia.[93] Naxagoras thinks that the Fleece was actually conquered by Jason, a necessary venture to give back to Greece what once was hers; for the story behind the fable is probably that Phrixos, after quarrelling with his mother-in-law, got hold of the treasure of his father Athamas and set off on a ship (*"Schiff"*) called "sheep" (*"Schaaf"*). Eventually, the treasure would have assumed the name of the ship. In the eighteenth century there was still a kind of ship called *"Schaaf,"* well-known to sailors. Naxagoras surveys, and at times extensively quotes several dictionaries and authors,[94] notably an abstract of one "Mirror of Alchemy," according to which this myth contains, behind the veil of story, an outline of the art's processes: the ram was none other than a parchment made of sheepskins and then covered with gold letters, because the text deals with gold, that is, with how to discover the hermetic secrets.[95]

Naxagoras adopts this interpretation, adding that the name of Jason's father can be spelled AEson, like the name of Virgil's hero, AEneas. Both words could be related to Hermes AES, which, as a matter of fact, is fould elsewhere in the book. AEson and AEneas have been restored to youth and have regained strength, the former by Medea who symbolizes hermetic medicine, the latter by the Sibyl and a golden bough. AEs (not related by the author to *AEsch*, fire, a Hebrew term, as in *AEsch Metzarereph*) is the Sun, or ferment, *sulphur fixum,* restored to youth by the Golden Fleece. "Medea" could mean "reflection" or "research," deriving from a word meaning the "beginning, the origin, or the source of a thing." This is Medea who taught Jason how to obtain the Golden Fleece, that is, transmutation, and also how to restore health in weakened bodies: such is the virtue of the philosophical AES. The alchemical Opus has its Medea, called Luna by the sages; her role is to put to sleep brazen-footed animals who send out dreadful flames through their nostrils. She is able to restore youth to old Demogoron, or Adam, or adamic soil, to restore his health, and also to cure all types of diseases; so much so that a man can reach a very advanced age, and live as long as God would permit, not to mention the riches that this man would derive from it. And Naxagaoras goes on to mention examples of several figures who lived a hundred years or even much longer. This magician Medea is to Jason somewhat as Dame Pernelle is to Nicolas Flamel. But she could no more be accused of being a witch than could Dame Pernelle. What would have been the point of Jason resorting to witchcraft? Neither would it be fair to accuse her of being cruel when she burned King Cremon to death or even when she killed her two children. She flew off to Athens on a chariot drawn by two dragons, meaning that she represents the Spiritus Mercurii flowing up the alembic. In Athens, she married King AEgeo, and bore him a son named Medium, that is, the "medium part of the art." In marrying Hypsiphilles, Jason was not at fault either; this marriage was not adultery, nor was it ingratitude towards Medea: it means that as matter gets transformed in the athanor, its name changes, for it must be 'married' several times.[96]

Naxagoras related the word "Vliess" (fleece) to *"fliessen"* (to flow) to point out the watery quality of the image besides its fiery nature. In a long and beautiful passage, he placed the emphasis on the verb *"vello, vellere"* (to take out, to pull out); for instance, *"vellere herbas"* (to pull out weeds). Before scissors were invented, sheep hairs were pulled out! From this would derive *"Wolle"* (wool): so *Vellus Aureum* is the golden wool taken from the Ram, "in whom the philosophic Sun is exalted." This matter used to prepare the philosophers' stone contains the three principles in a state of extreme purification. So here we are talking about a substance which would be, if I am correctly interpreting Naxagoras' somewhat involved explanations, midway between ordinary or gross substances and a glorified or philosophers' state of matter. Hermes Trismegistus, whom Naxagoras here quotes as his authority, reminds us through his teaching and his very name that besides the four elements there are also three principles in "one and the same holy stone." As a matter of fact, the Ram's skin "is none other than Hermes' Emerald Tablet, for the reason that upon this tablet the whole art has been described in summary." Whether this text was engraved on emerald or on a skin is immaterial; it was, in any case, of such value as to be placed only "in the hands of kings and princes who understood the art."[97] (cf. *infra,* Appendix 1, #6).

Further on, Naxagoras related our myth to the Egyptian Emerald Tablet, in connection with Seneca's Democrites (mentioned in Seneca's letter 90): Democrites is said to know how to soften ivory and to make emeralds grow in size (cf. *infra,* Appendix 1, #7):

> Democrites, in particular, a man of remarkable intellect, felt prompted to go to Egypt to learn about the mysteries of Nature and the true Philosophy. He secretly opened the burial chamber of the Egyptian priest Dardanus, and found beside him the books de-

scribing the Golden Philosophy or the hidden mysteries of Nature, namely the *Aureum Vellus*. He brought them to Greece. He studied them, and finally wrote books himself on alchemy that have survived, about the coloring of gold, silver, and stones.

A reference to the tomb is noteworthy, for in 1717, in Nuremberg, a new *Tumba Semiramidis Hermeticae Sigillatae* had been published, in the wake of several *Tumbae* of that type, also ascribed to Democrites of Abdere. The author notes that Jason was not the first nor the only one to set off on a journey in order to learn the art. Moreover, it may be that the kings of Egypt fled to Colchis, bringing with them some of their hermetic books; which is why, as Suidas writes, Diocletian had the books of the Egyptians burnt, so they could not become rich at his expense.[98] References to the Egyptians are not infrequent in this book. Naxagoras believes that Pythagoras was probably indebted to them for his doctrine of the transmigration of souls, a subject about which, however, he seems to have a different understanding. By transmigration it should be understood that in the first stage of the work, the soul of gold moves into the alchemical Moon—its ram—and that afterward the souls of both move into the sign of Taurus, and that all three then move into Gemini. According to the three operations of the preliminary work, the stone is first animal, then becomes vegetable through Aries and mineral through Taurus; only then do the Sun and the Moon appear. By all accounts, those Egyptians were alchemists. Their Emerald Tablet itself was designed in a way reminiscent of the laboratory process of vitrification (cf. *infra*, Appendix 1, # 8):

> Vitrum is one of the things that help in the preparation, for it is through the reduction of iron into *vitrum preparatum* that all the residual particles of matter can be removed, thus allowing one to proceed to the next stages. No one can go easily into the deeper and secret meaning of what is said here without a faithful Master. That is why Hermes himself rightly thought of writing the art on an emerald not unlike a beautiful blue sapphire of the size of a tablet; he wished thereby to indicate that the entire art is based on this green or sapphire color. In Hermes, it is green; in the prophet Isaiah, it is sapphire. Upon the Tablet of Hermes is written: "And just as all things proceed from one alone who thought of them, so also proceed and spring forth all things (which belong to the art) from this one thing which brings together the most worthy part through a way or a disposition." Similarly, the true philosophers all advise that no foreign elements should be added to it.[99]

Naxagoras establishes a dazzling array of correspondences between the alchemical process and mythology. For instance, the thick cloud with which Jupiter covered Io represents the film that appears during the coagulation of the elixir. Like Proteus, Argus' eyes represent sulphur when turning from black to other colors. The Gorgon suggests that fixing quality of the elixir. Numerous other examples could be given. While analyzing the alchemical symbology of the myth, Naxagoras discussed several characters. The dragon guarding the Fleece is, in a way, its golden wool. Cadmus wants to slay him: the creature must be put to sleep so that it stops belching fire and smoke. To this end, it is suffocated in water, that is, dissolved, in order to be robbed of the volatile and the fixed hidden in his center—and thereafter those who, with Jason, seek the art, have nothing more to do than conquer the Fleece and restore old AEson to youth. Such is the purpose of the next work, as indicated by Medea. AEson is none other than a soil, the pure element of which has been extracted. Cadmus is devoured by the dragon, and their two souls become one: after the preparation of the chaos, nothing but mercurial water should be sought in it. The awakened dragon is a white and red liquid fire through which Nature acts; it is the one and only root of all minerals and metals, the golden seed, and he who knows it possesses the roots of life and finds his way to that place he yearns for. In this dragon there is the fountain of life, the salt of the transfigured body. Its teeth sowed in the earth (which then turn into armed men intent on defending the Fleece) speak of a secret that should not be disclosed: at this point, Naxagoras says he is unwilling to break the divine mirror through indiscretion.[100]

An idea found occasionally in the book, and already present in the title itself, is that of concordance (*Concordanz*). It is a matter of making a comparative survey of the views of the ancients in order to draw from them a doctrine that could be called the "tradition." As early as 1606, Franz Kieser used the word in that sense,[101] and other alchemists had probably done so before him. Jason, Naxagoras explained, followed the guidance of the wise Medea, who gave him the means to carry through his venture, even though there were trials and hardships (cf. *infra,* Appendix 1, # 9):

He succeeded after a hazardous voyage on the philosophical sea, which represents the study and reading of the philosophers' writings. These writings are like an unfathomable ocean, and rough, upon which no one could keep his course without a compass—that is, without the understanding of the concordance. Indeed, this journey is fraught with countless dangers because of the dragons we have told about, of the lions and other monsters; it is itself the studious research and the uncertain experience of the things of the art; it is the preparation thereof, where many spend most of their lives, unable to reach the longed-for haven of this great ocean. And it is, in truth, a meaningful poetic device to communicate something of the actual art under the veil of history. To ordinary people, it gives an impression of the bizarre, they see strange and unheard-of tales, or even something to be laughed at, in what is to us quite a common and well-known thing. What I say here is in agreement with Henricus Madathanus, also known as *Hadrian at Mynsicht.*[102]

We could never properly understand the Holy Scriptures without 'combining its concordances.' The same goes for law. And what are Hippocrates' 'aphorisms' but the concordance of a variety of medical observations, first compiled in the temple of Aesculapius? Without a concordance, we become lost in a maze of inhuman observations and experiences, as is the case with countless alchemists working haphazardly. Naxagoras believes, as a corollary, that myths may be interrelated so that we can find in them common denominators pregnant with meaning. In the last chapter, he quotes a great many authorities, and finally demonstrates that "concordance" virtually means what we now call "tradition."[103]

Let us close with a fine image he gives us. Raymond Lull had promised to the King of England a bell whose ringing would be heard throughout the world—at least through Europe. Lull dropped a particle of his alchemical tincture into the molten brass, and as a result the whole bell turned into gold. It never did ring, probably because it was used for other purposes; but the story itself was heard echoing everywhere, up to this day. The same may be said about Argo: the wood used for the construction of this ship came from a forest of speaking trees, and so Argo was able to speak; as a matter of fact, it is still speaking today, but its tale is told through a great number of human tongues.[104]

THEOSOPHICAL FLEECE AND ASTRAL GOLD: HERMANN FICTULD; THE "SUN FROM THE ORIENT"

We have essentially no more information about Hermann Fictuld than we have about Naxagoras. Elsewhere I have written about Hermann Fictuld and his discussion of the Order founded by Philip the Good.[105] He had probably read his predecessor's book, and mentions his full name, while freely criticizing this colleague adept in hermetic sciences.[106] Fictuld's *Aureum Vellus* was published in 1749; as far as I know this is the only alchemical work entirely devoted to our myth. We learn about this exclusiveness even from the title itself: *Aureum Vellus or Golden Fleece: wherein is explained its true nature, as well as its origin and its greatness. Drawn from ancient texts, offered to the sons of the art and to the lovers of hermetic philosophy; wherein it is clearly shown that it conceals the Prima Materia Philosophorum and its praxis. With helpful explanatory notes.*[107]

No one, he states at the outset, has so far fully elucidated the myth of the Golden Fleece. Its exponents have only aroused our desire to learn more about it.[108] And Fictuld goes on to name them, at least those that came to his notice through treatises mentioning the word in their titles: Aloisius Marlianus, Giovanni Aurelio Augurelli, Johann Conrad Creiling, Ehrd of Naxagoras, Johannes de Monte Hermetis, Guilielmus Mennens, and in addition the collection of texts published in Rorschach in 1598, and Johann Siebmacher's own collection (whose name he mentions only indirectly). The list ends there.[109]

This, says Fictuld, is the tale of a 'hermetic alphabet.'[110] The Fleece represents the liquid, astral gold, extracted from the nature of higher realities and from the elements; as a soul and seed, as a solar substance flowing out of God's bounty, it gives life to things, sustains them, and is able to penetrate the most dense and solid bodies.[111] That is why Philip the Good chose it as the symbol of his chivalric Order, which is indeed the only one in the West to bear a name derived from paganism and to be presided over by the Great Art.[112]

Just as the great coronation ceremonies followed a sacred ritual bearing witness to the glory of God and the honor of man, so also the Golden Fleece was for Philip the indispensable royal garb of the high science.[113] Fictuld writes at length about this Order; since I have written about most of the many alchemical interpretations he gives to it I refer the reader to my work.[114]

We should be aware that everything Fictuld says, everything he sees, weaves an alchemical and theosophical web, wherein the destiny of Man and Nature interconnect. After Adam's fall, God gave him, in His providence and mercy, notwithstanding the curse laid upon everything on earth, a remedy still to be found at the center of plants and even minerals, a medicine that could keep men in good health, save them from their passions, and cure nature.[115] Adam had not fallen as low as his descendants, who were to be chastised by the flood; so he had no need for an interpreter or a hermeneutist (*Textausleger*) in order to understand the words of the Lord or those of Nature: he just 'saw' them, as if in a mirror, and passed on to his children whatever knowledge he retained. Some of them became its custodians, even after the Flood, such as Haspar, son of Japhet and grandson of Noah; he was lifted up to the seventh Heaven, and like Hermes was well-versed in the 'mercurial' arts and sciences. However, these arts remained secret to prevent their falling into impure hands which would have used them to increase evil in the world.[116]

At this point in his theosophical discourse, Fictuld brings in the myth of the Golden Fleece which, as we have seen, should be read as a 'hermetic alphabet'. About two years before our era and 2700 years after the creation of the world, in the days of the Judges of Israel, Athamas reigned over Thebes. His wife Nephelea bore him two children, Phrixos and Helle. Athamas was high-spirited; Nephele of melancholic disposition (cf. *infra*, Appendix 1, # 10):

> Nephele gave to her children the golden book or scroll made, according to the custom of the times, out of sheep skins or ram skins. A long scroll like those still used today by the Jews to write down the Mosaic law, the Prophets, and the Psalms. According to ancient custom it bore signs: golden figures, symbols, letters, and pictures—the sublime art and science of the ancients. Not only the art of making gold, but also all seven sciences of the sublime wisdon, of Magia, of the Cabbala, and of astronomy. This scroll was kept as a testamentary gift in the royal closet, and the children had to get hold of it and flee to some remote country in the wilderness, or to their cousins', that is, to their mother's brother's, the King of Colchis, in Georgia or Mingrelia, now called Odisey.[117]

The children had to flee because Ino (Cadmus' daughter, whom Athamas had subsequently married) wanted to kill them. So they fled from Thebes with the golden scroll, on a ship called the Golden Fleece! Helle died during the crossing, and her body was committed to the ocean. Phrixos reached Colchis, where he married the king's daughter; became a king in his turn; had two children, including prince AEtha, Medea's father. Later on, AEson reigned in Thessalia, and his heir, Jason, set off to Colchis: there he escaped a plot fostered by priests and court counsellors—the two fire-spitting dragons!—because of Medea who helped him to poison them. Jason brought to Thebes the scroll, this great treasure upon which is written the art of making gold along with other wonderful secrets.[118]

We owe the *Emerald Tablet* to our 'patriarch Hermes'[119] and Fictuld has provided a lengthy hermeneutics of it on at least two occasions. The other exegesis is to be found in this *Turba Philosophorum* (1763), where there is no mention of the Golden Fleece. So let us turn to what he tells us in *Aureum Vellus*. First, the initial line of the famous *Tablet* teaches: "As above, so below; as below, so above." This means that the matter of our stone is here below, upon this earth, in this treasure chamber of the underworld, symbolized by the realm of Colchis. The stone is like that which is above, that is, in the celestial elements and the sidereal parts, symbolized by the realm of Thebes. Both realms are one and the same polarized Centrum, like an active-passive pair (man-woman or seed-field), and therefore generate the 'royal children.'[120] "To accomplish the miracle of one thing": the beginning of the *Opus* is a single thing wherein lie all those things of which the world consists. It is a mercurial sulphur and a sulphurous mercury; that is, a fiery water or a watery fire. If it is thus separated from fire and water, and if both elements are then combined in such a way that the water turns into a solid and the stone into a liquid, the secret of the art will have been found.[121] The *Emerald Tablet* further says: "And just as all things proceed from one alone, by will and command of one alone who conceive of it . . ." All that is in the world, according to Fictuld's interpretation, proceeds from a *Materia* or chaos, or *Primum Ens,* arising from the divine breath turned into water (cf. also Fictuld's treatise *Azoth and Ignis,* published at the same time as *Aureum Vellus*). Other alchemical elucidations follow,[122] but we limit ourselves to those that make use of the Golden Fleece. The text goes on: "The sun is its father, the moon is its mother, the wind has borne it in its womb, its nurse is the earth." Touching here upon a different level, Fictuld comments that Hermes brings us closer to the goal, makes us understand how matter is generated in the higher realm, how it is born upon the earth, what this matter actually is, and finally how to treat it to bring it to its perfection. Then Fictuld offers us the following scenario:

Athamas (or the sun, sulphur) is the father of Phrixos and Helle, that is, of the androgynous child mentioned in the *Emerald Tablet.* These two children represent respectively "a solar sulphur and a lunar mercury." They are generated by the igneous semen flowing into Nephelea's womb (the mother, or the moon). After gestation within the mother, Phrixos and Helle do not remain in these higher regions—symbolized by the city of Thebes—but go down to earth, charged with the igneous qualities of their father, and with their mother's mercurial qualities. A comparison borrowed from real nature and drawn from Paracelsus gives us a clue. The sun, Fictuld says, does not send out his rays directly upon the earth; first he focuses them on the moon, who "takes away their heat" and thus prevents our planet from being scorched. But Fictuld goes beyond this 'physical' comparison of the myth of the two children: he offers a markedly theosophical reading. There are two reasons, he explains, why Phrixos and Helle cannot stay in Thebes, a higher region and their birthplace. First, Nephelea, the moon, is too weak and cold to keep the fruit of her union with Athamas, the sun. And then, some evil influence—characterized by the author as jupiterian, 'arsenical', and which, strangely enough, he connects with the harmful action of the priests—drives this progeny out of the celestial regions and forces them, like a rain symbolized by the Ram or his fleece, to go down to earth, symbolized by the realm of Colchis; that is down into the four elements and the three principles of which our earthly nature consists.

Reading a few lines further, we learn that Ino, Athamas' second wife, may be taken as the embodiment of this evil influence. She is indeed the instrument for the 'arsenical' negative influence that the demons, or angels who followed Lucifer during the first breach of trust, continue to exercise in the universe. Portrayed by the Greek myth as a cruel stepmother, a usurper, she typifies the evil force "created, slipped in, inserted, as a secondary element by the frightening curse of God only after the fall of Lucifer and Adam." This is a supremely evil force, a destructive agent, presiding over the two processes of death brought about by the original fall: on the one hand, the transformation of a "large area" (meaning the universe prior to the original disaster brought about by Lucifer) into a "contemptible desert"; on the other hand, the sudden descent of both children, symbolized by Phrixos and Helle, to this desert.

The setting, the scenario, the tone, and at times even the vocabulary, already belong to eighteenth century Illuminism. We find them again in Fictuld's contemporary, Saint-Georges de Marsais, and also in others; Saint-Martin uses them extensively. In spite of his chaotic exposition and his inflated style, Fictuld's discourse is quite clear if only we take the trouble to analyze it. Of the myth of Phrixos and Helle, which cannot be separated here from that of the *Emerald Tablet,* he gives us an interesting reading, for it goes through three different and complementary levels. First, there is the classical story of the fall of Man: Adam and Eve (Phrixos and Helle) fallen from the celestial regions, still retain something of their former glory. "The wind" has borne them "in its womb" to nourish them, and then to drive them down to earth. Second, we have here a cosmosophy, since this line ("The wind has borne him in its womb") is understood as an ever-flowing and fecundating cosmic energy (arising from the union of a solar and a lunar principle) pouring down upon the earth, obliquely so as not to "burn" it, and therefore first deflected to a "moon" which acts as a damping device and a prism. Third, we are of course dealing with an alchemical text. Since there is, in Man and in nature, a hidden substance which came down from the celestial regions (or, depending on the context, the positive residue of a state that was before the fall) the question is how to isolate it, then to work on it in order to turn it into the philosophers' stone. The spark buried deep in our hearts and in nature's heart yearns to become a life-giving fire.

The whole passage is written in a strange language, more rococo than baroque (it is given *in extenso* in Appendix 1, # 11). There is extensive use of such ideas as 'arsenical' spirit, active sulphur, passive mercury, and the third principle salt, typified here by the ambiguous role given to the moon. The idea of the rays drawing their seed, or their higher essence, from the union of salt and moon, then of the seed being sown upon the earth, reaching the center, is in line with the categories of Paracelcism and was aptly elaborated upon by a Franciscus Kieser with the same flexibility in his *Cabala Chymica* published in Frankfurt in 1606.[123]

The text of the *Emerald Tablet* goes on: "It is the father of the perfection in the whold world; its power will come in full (*vollkommen*) if it is converted into earth."[124] What may be understood thereby is that AEson is the great king, the philosophic root, the mineral of the sages, the metal of the ancient Philosophers. Where does he reign? In Thessalia, that is, upon the earth, a speck of dust in the vast universe. Adam is *The-S-Salia,* which means particles of solar sulphur. God created him immortal through a substance, and extract in the universe pertaining to all creatures; in other words, a quintessence of all juices and energies existing in it, while creatures prior to him had been made only out of God's will and breath. Lucifer, who was responsible for the fall, was, like every angel, made from the pure and fiery waters of the first separation.[125]

"Thou shalt separate the earth from fire, the subtle from the gross, with much care and industry. It rises from earth to heaven and comes down again to earth, and thus acquires the power of the realities above and the realities below." This means that the subtle fire of the elements lies hidden in water (in the alembic and vessels spiritualized matter flows up), and then must come down again into earth, whose soul or life is water. When water has separated from earth, the latter is nothing more than a dead body; to generate, it needs its anima, its life, its spirit—its water. Here we are told of a double marriage: water makes earth more fluid, more subtle; earth makes water thicker, more fixed, more corporeal. Earth is Colchis; when rightly prepared, it releases the Golden

Fleece.[126]

The *Emerald Tablet* says that separation must be achieved softly. Here again the example of Medea gives us a clue, Fictuld notes. For Medea does not steal nor take away forcibly, but uses coaxing, ceremonies. The two fire-spitting dragons represent the saturnian and arsenical influences, cold and dry. Historically, they must be the ministers of state, or the counsellors of the court of Colchis. Medea offered them a liquor that killed them, just as the Cerberuses were overcome by an 'oriental soup'. Those two dragons have become ingredients of the philosophers' stone, just as the tail of the Lernaean Hydra is said to have been used as theriaca. The Golden Fleece itself, as a male seed, must first dissolve into the seed of the moon, and then coagulate; it produces the same result as the union of mercury and sulphur, namely a cinnabar. This is because mercury's principle comes from earth and water, while sulphur's principle comes from earth and fire.[127]

Next came, in 1758, Pernety's *Fables,* which in spite of their one-sided interpretations, have remained a source of interest up to this day. However, they have not been accepted in every circle, far from it. In Germany, though people knew of them, they left hardly any trace. Witness a strange book in German published in the late period of the Enlightenment: no mention here of the French Benedictine, although it deals at length with the Golden Fleece, here again introduced by a drawing and an elucidation of the collar of the chivalric Order. The title could be rendered as follows: *The Sun from the Orient, or a philosophical interpretation of the collar of the Golden Fleece; as well as of the cross of the Order of the Knights Templars, the Johannite, Teutonic Knights, and so forth, with some cabbalistic figures and a mirror of touchstone of the philosophic matter, together with a special interpretation thereof for its friends, sons of wisdom,* 1783.[128]

Philip the Good, the anonymous author declares, possessed the philosophers' stone, whether he found it himself or received it from an adept. Indeed, this commentator's approach to the collar's symbolism, holding that the whole secret of the hermetic art is contained in the myth of Jason, is quite original. In the flintstones he distinguishes the steel elements proper, or *"acies"* (*Staale*), and sees there a symbol of the twofold philosophic matter, as found by the artist in its "raw" state. Many authors are quoted in this respect. Rhasis teaches: *"materia est unica, attamen duplex."* For Bernardus Trevisanus, the work starts from one single root and two mercurial substances: sulphur (hot and dry) corresponds to the collar's flintstones, and mercury (cold and humid) to its steel. The *Turba Philosophorum* joins in marriage the red man (the flintstones) with the woman (the steel) in a white bedroom.

Sendivogius speaks of one matter in two substances: gold and steel, or again quickgold and quicksilver. According to Hermes it is made up of a red sulphur and a white mercury. For Pierre Lombard (Pietro d'Abano?) it appears to be made of liquid substance and thick substance, mixed together. Still other authorities are quoted to convince us of this polarity, expressed through the pairs of opposite Lion/Snake, winged and non-winged dragon, sun and moon, fixed and volatile, and also to remind us that the union of both terms results in *rebis,* or *res bina.*

There follows an account of the great black stone used here as a pendant and linking the chain of flintstones to the ram. This black stone (cf. figure XI) is adorned with seven red drops, or tears of fire, representing the seven houses of the fiery water, together with the connection between the seven planets and metals. The ram itself is the matter produced through the joining of the flintstones with the steel. His skin must be removed to find inside his body the flesh and the blood, that is, Sendivogius says, the sulphur or golden fire contained in his stomach, just as fire is kindled from the stones through the steel. With his golden wool this animal symbolizes also the perfected matter, the gold tincture or the philosophers' stone, completed in the sign of Aries, that sign in which the Work was started. Indeed, we may choose either the dry or the humid path, but it is always better to start in March, when the sun enters this sign, for through this astral gold everything on earth begins to sprout, including what is inside our athanor! Our anonymous author also sees here, in this connection between Mars and Aries, the origin of Eastern red eggs, related to some form of divine magic

FRENCH EXEGESES: DOM PERNETY OR THE GROUP WITH A SINGLE KEY; FULCANELLI AT THE HOTEL LALLEMANT; CANSELIET AND CABBALISTIC PHONETICS

Less than ten years after Fictuld's book, two works by Dom Pernety, a Benedictine of Saint-Maur, were published in 1758: the *Dictionnaire Mytho-Hermétique* and *Les Fables Egyptiennes et Grecques dévoilées et réduites au même principe.* For the most part, it is the latter, with its sixty pages or so devoted to the Golden Fleece, which is of interest to us. There is no need for a detailed introduction to Dom Pernety, who is a very well-known figure. Besides being a Benedictine, he served as librarian at the Berlin Royal Library, accompanied Bougainville to the Falkland islands, and, in Avignon, led a group of Illuminati gathered in a "Hermetic Rite."[129] Besides references to the records of antiquity, a few alchemical texts from the Middle Ages and the Renaissance, and the contemporary research in mythology, Pernety barely mentions exegeses of the myth of Jason. He seems unaware of most of the German texts on the subject. His grasp of ancient culture, however, is stupendous, and his alchemical readings are substantial and classic. Among the mythographers of his day, his chosen target was the celebrated Antoine Banier, who wrote *La Mythologie et les Fables expliquées par l'histoire,* the publication of which began in 1711.[130]

According to Banier, and his thoroughly euhemeristic exegesis, one should not look for the secrets of the Greek Work in mythology, either in the story or the Argonauts of in the rest of the myths.[131] Moreover, he admits that he does not quite understand how the fables could distort historical and geographical reality to the point of making it hardly recognizable. Pernety addresses himself to an explanation: the fables were written as a cover for the description of the alchemical processes. Throughout his extensive book, Pernety stresses this point so much that never for a moment does he appear to ask himself if there might exist some autonomous activity of the creative imagination, free from any teaching or demonstrative purpose.

Behind the distortions placed by the fables upon 'reality,' the Benedictine looks for one message only, one referring to the chrysopoeia in its more concrete, 'operative' aspects. Most of the 'mistakes' found in poets like Homer, Orpheus, Apollonios of Rhodes, etc., seem to him "to serve a purpose, as if to indicate that what they tell us are pure fictions and not real stories"[139]—fictions with a very precise content, especially as Pernety always appears to believe that their authors, because they made such conscious and deliberate efforts, did not want to leave anything to chance. They were discharging a sacred duty: the poets' doctrine was one they had received from the priests of Egypt; it was "the philosophy of Hermes, or the sacerdotal art, henceforth known as hermetic art."[133] Indeed, it is from the priests of Egypt themselves "that Orpheus, Apollonius, and many others had learned about the way that should be walked to attain the goal in the practice of this art"; thus, if the geography of the Argonauts' return, for instance, is in contradiction with cartography, this is only because it is not a description of earth but of the Great Work.[134] Pernety goes on to formulate this proposition, essential for his purpose, and such an approach, had it been less monolithic, could have taken him much further than he actually went: "If we were finally to compare all mythological stories with one another, we would easily realize that I am correct in reducing all of them to one single principle, because they really have but one object."[135]

In writing this way, Pernety does not pause to consider whether he is not himself falling into the reductionist bias for which he severely criticizes other mythologists like Thomassin and Huet, "who tried to reduce most of the mythological stories to those found in the Bible," and who believed these fables to be "the stories of Abraham, Agar and Sara, of Moses and Josuah." Truly, he thinks, "if we accept such ideas, there is no mythological story, no matter how tangibly mythological, that cannot be brought in line with them." He also censures Le Clerc, who saw in the Argonautic expedition "the mere account of a journey, an illicit trading venture of Greek merchants on the eastern shores of the Euxine."[136] Pernety is concerned with enlightening us; to this end he frequently uses a method of rhetoric which accumulates a series of questions, the answers to which cannot be doubted by any sensible mind, thus leaving his readers with no alternative interpretations but his own.[137]

Moreover, his correlations between Golden Fleece and chryso-poeia are not very innovative. We have already come across examples like these in other writers. The originality of his work lies in its unusual breadth: no one before him had devoted so many pages to the interpretation of Greek and Egyptian myths in terms of operative alchemy exclusively. Here are a few examples. We find again the thesis of Jason's two masters: Cheiron, who was already the teacher of Hercules and Achilles, for the theory, and Medea for practice and guidance. If Jason lands in Lemnos to propitate Vulcan, this is because without him and with only Neptune, that is, with water and without fire, the adept is powerless. The unbearable stench of the women of Lemnos signifies the putrefied and rotten matter at the bottom of the vessel. The murder of their husbands signifies the dissolution of the fixed through the agency of the volatile.[138] Phineas' food being persistently taken away by the Harpies signifies a process of volatilization. These Harpies are in the form of females "in order to point out their flightiness, since, as an ancient said: *Quid levius fumo? flamen. Quid flamine? ventus. / Quid vento? mulier. Quid muliere? nihil.*" This touch of misogyny strikes us as a pleasant diversion in the middle of a lengthy enumeration. Having been chased away, the Harpies are confined "in the Isle of Plote (that is, floating or swimming) because matter, when it coagulates, forms a floating island."[139] To send a dove over the Symplegades is "to volatilize matter."[140] Pulling out the dragon's teeth means extracting "the seed of the philosophers' gold, which thereafter must be sowed."[141] As for the Fleece, "Mercury has gilded it, since citrine, a color midway between white and rust, is produced by mercury."[142] Pernety also makes a relevant comparison between Ariadne and Medea, and concludes that "these two fictions are one and the same thing, explained through allegories, the circumstances of which have been purposely diversified, to make them appear as two different stories."[143] Here the word "purposely" is typical! As a matter of fact, his parallels are often interesting, for instance when he relates Cheiron's living on Mount Pelion to the construction of Argo, made of wood from that mountain.[144] Finally, the attempt to reduce everything to the chrysopoeia forces him to reach out for some kind of synthesis, occasionally with remarkable and stimulating results, although not necessarily at all in line with what he meant to achieve. In addition, his efforts result in fine passages like the following:

> The oak used for the construction of this ship is the same against which Cadmus killed the snake who had devoured his companions; it is that hollow oak, with the rose tree of Abraham the Jew planted at its foot, about which Flamel writes; that same oak again is standing close to the fountain of Trevisan, and mentioned by Espagnet in Canon 114 of his Treatise. The trunk of this oak must therefore be hollow; which is why it was called a ship. And Typhis has been pictured as one of the pilots, because fire is the pilot of the work [. . .]. He was given Ancea for assistant, to indicate that this fire must be like that of a hen sitting on its eggs, as the philosophers put it.[145]

In the three columns of his *Dictionnaire Mytho-Hermétique* devoted to Jason, Pernety refers the reader to this work, but also returns to certain themes: Why did Euripyle present Jason with some earth? "Because Euripyle was Neptune's son, because out of water earth is made, and out of this earth water must be made." Again, there was some purpose behind the fact that Phineas was delivered from the Harpies by two sons of Aeolus, "since Basilius Valentinus says in the sixth Key that two winds must blow, one being the eastern wind, which he calls *Vulturnus,* and the other the southern wind, or *Notus.* When these two winds have abated, the harpies will be put to flight, that is, the volatile parts will become fixed.[146] Q.E.D.!

Approximately fifteen years later, the adept Denis Molinier shows the same concerns. His manuscript, written in the seventies and never published, appears as a commentary of Abraham the Jew's famous *Livre des figures hiéroglyphiques.* Dependent upon a longstanding tradition, Molinier has included in his manuscript a chapter entitled "L'explication des fables par l'alchimie et l'oeuvre des philosophes hermétiques."[147] The approach and the main idea are the same. Molinier practices variations on perfectly similar motifs. However, he is not plagiarizing Pernety but, rather, attempting to make new comparisons:

Jason (. . .) consults the medicine of the enchantress Medea because it is quite natural that the (Sulphur) of nature *personified in Jason* seeks its other half (Mercury) to overcome the obstacle it has to face for its perfecting and becoming elixir (. . .); so Jason comes out of Medea, and both the lover and the mistress are but one single thing to accomplish our work in uniting in elixir. However, to reveal our secret without restriction, it is good to let you know that this lover and this mistress, this male and this female, are themselves made up of several substances, and that they have been made through various operations of our art (. . . .) Jason is also a (Sulphur) spirit like Persea, only much more perfect than he, for the latter is as much fixed as the other is volatile; and anyone wishing to enjoy it must have recourse to Minerva, the mother of science, and to Medea, the consort of experiment, for it requires some peculiar skills to unite spirits and join them through a contract of eternal marriage, so that they turn into fixed and permanent (Sulphur), called philosophers' stone of the Golden Fleece, conquered by Jason (. . . .) We understand Medea as this (Sulphur) of nature of the third kind, for then it is our medea, that is, medicine fit for any disease and therefore the key to any medicine or natural magic, and the foundation of religion and of the Kabbala, about which we have already said many great things (. . . .)"[148]

Louis-Claude de Saint-Martin may have had Pernety in mind while composing his *Tableau Naturel* published in 1782, and therefore probably written at the same time as Molinier's alchemical texts.[149] It is not concerned with the Golden Fleece, but his criticism of those alchemists who interpret mythology should be noted here in view of its interest and its source: Louis-Claude de Saint-Martin was one of the greatest theosophers (cf. *infra,* Appendix 1, # 12). Here, he explains, the hermetic art does not reach beyond material objects; it does not belong to a higher class than agriculture. It is wrong to attribute to material operations the principles relating to objects of a far superior class, and described under the veil of mythology. But to explain such objects by alchemy is to disparage this mythology instead of explaining it to us. What should be read in ancient myths is the true 'science of man', that science which tells us about our origins, our ultimate purpose, about the laws which lead us to our goal, and about the causes that keep us away from it.

In 1839, Franz von Baader, another of these very great modern theosophers, welcomes Saint-Martin's refutation of this explanation of mythology through the hermetic art. Saint-Martin did not mention the names of the authors he had in mind, but Baader mentions three: Jacob Tollius, for his 1687 *Fortuita;* Michael Maier, for his 1610 *Arcana Arcanissima;* and Pernety, for his 1758 *Dictionnaire.* It has been said, Baader explains, that the ancient fables should be understood as a multi-faceted picture that would represent the 'living fire of Nature'. This is an interesting idea, but the ennobling of metals and the healing of bodies are achievements which do not go 'beyond time'. One cannot speak of true 'higher physics' except in regard to a man who is himself totally involved in the process of his own transmutation. And this is why the true object of the mythological traditions is the science of the early history of humanity: the science of what humanity was, of what it is, of what it will be—the science of the relation of Man with God, and with the universe.[150] Unlike Saint-Martin, Baader considers alchemy to be a royal art. That is why he criticizes Pernety's interpretations, not because he thinks they are wrong, as Saint-Martin believes, but because they are confined to the same, the most material, level.

Pernety's conundrum is at the same time a swan song; henceforth, the Golden Fleece is seldom mentioned in hermetic writing. On the other hand, it hardly comes as a surprise to see the Ram and Jason introduced by Freemasonry in some of its rites. In themselves, both figures are sufficiently evocative of initiation to justify this choice, and too closely related to the very notion of chivalry to be overlooked by the rituals of the time, with their proliferation of chivalric grades. Since the appearance of Freemasonry's Higher Grades, around 1740, and up to this day, the rites borrowing from this myth draw from the alchemical symbology, and the lodges practising those rites appeal to people fond of alchemy. Thus, while the alchemical interpretation of the Golden Fleece becomes a rarity from Pernety's writings through the twentieth century, this hermetic reading of the myth is carried on, at least in part, within the lodges. A note on this issue is appended to the present study (Appendix 2).

Apart from a few hints in the nineteenth century alchemical texts which I consulted, I did not find any passages on the Golden Fleece worth mentioning here; however, this does not mean they are non-existent.[151]

Since we cannot fill this gap right now, let us skip over that century. We will not be disappointed with the twentieth century, with its two masters of high renown among both adepts and general public: Fulcan-elli and Canseliet. Like Dom Pernety they are French; but their reading of alchemy is richer than the Benedictine's, for it is much more diversi-fied, complex, and in no way confined to simplistic patterns. The En-lightenment is far behind, the days of scientism—and therefore of occultism—are almost over. How similar are these two authors!—so much so that it has been suspected they might be one and the same person: the disciple Canseliet, under the name Fulcanelli, might have fabricated for himself both a master and a pseudonym.[159]

Fulcanelli's *Le mystère des cathédrales*,[153] published in 1925, leads us also into various 'philosophers' houses', one of which is relevant here: a mansion built in Bourges around 1500, the Hôtel Lallemant, already mentioned above. After showing us around the dining hall, with its panelled ceiling and its high mantelpiece bearing the arms of Louis XI and Ann of Britanny, Fulcanelli beckons us into the chapel containing the splendid bas-relief which prompts a few reflections: "The fable of the Golden Fleece," he writes, "is a cryptic story of the whole hermetic work, which is to produce the philosophers' stone. In the language of the adepts, the Golden Fleece refers to the matter prepared for the work, together with the final result. This is perfectly accurate, since these substances vary only in purity, fixedness and maturity."[154] The main difficulty "lies in the interpretation of the symbolism." So let us attempt to discern the truth under the veil of two distinct images: that of the oak, the initial subject, and that of the ram, whose two different aspects represent the same thing. The oak is "the initial subject, such as found in the mine." Admittedly, our author does not bring us much light, although it would surely be helpful in this mine. Fulcanelli is well aware of this, and adds: "The sentence we employ may seem ambiguous; we regret this, but we cannot be clearer without going beyond certain limits." The oak, he adds, often bears on its leaves a rough, round little outgrowth called "gall" (in Latin, "*galla*"), a word he derives from "gallus," "Gaul," in English, "cock"—the emblem of Gaul and Mercury's attribute. The oak also provides the "*kermes*," but while gall gives its name to the raw mercurial matter, kermes (in arabic *girmiz*, that which dyes scarlet) denotes the prepared substance. Now, "the philosophers' mercury, that is, their prepared matter, must acquire the power of dyeing, which it does but with the help of primal preparations."[155] So much for the object of the work. As for its subject, it is said to be "sometimes the magnetic and attracting quality of sulphur, sometimes its melting quality, sometimes its easy liquefaction." It is called *Magnesia Lunarii* or *Lead of the Sages,* and has still other names. It is a mineral corresponding to the astrological sign of the Ram. Then Fulcanelli closes with a synthetic shortcut, which is quite typical of him, wherein the elusive shimmers of lunar poetry set aglow a prism of intertwined symbols:

"*Gala,*" in Greek, means "milk," and mercury is also called

Virgin's Milk (*lac Virginis*). Therefore, brothers, if you remember what we have said about the Twelfth-night cake, and if you know why the Egyptians divinized the cat, you will be left in no doubt about the topic you should select; its common name will be clearly known to you. Then you will possess the chaos of the sages "wherein lie potentially all the hidden secrets," as Philalethes declares, and which the skillful artist promptly activates. Open up, that is, break down, such matter, try to isolate its pure portion, or its metallic soul, as they say, and you will have the Kermes, the Hermes, the 'tinging mercury' that holds the mystic gold, just as Saint Christopher carries Jesus and the ram his own fleece. You will come to understand why the Golden Fleece hangs to the oak, like the gall and the kermes, and you will be able to say without offending the truth that the old hermetic oak acts as a mother to the secret mercury. Comparing legends and symbols, some light will come to your mind and you will know the close affinity binding the oak to the ram, Saint Christopher to the Child-King, the Good Shepherd to the Sheep, a Christian counterpart of the criophorus (i.e., ram-bearer) Hermes, etc [156]

Here is a tantalizing morsel for an anthology. Beyond its interest as another document on the Golden Fleece, it also illustrates how *alchymia aeterna* is inclined to burn the reader alive in the crucible of its redundancies, to dazzle him with volleys of fireworks. In the face of this determined fire, we are left with three non-exclusive alternatives. We can try to understand the material, no matter how unequal to the task we may feel, with the expectation of finding, if not a stone, at least a pebble of wisdom. Or we can surrender to this strong current in the hopes that our active imagination, in cooperation with the unconscious, will perform some miracle. Or, finally, we can relish this discourse as a literary text, and then analyze it and articulate its structure.

On this point, the disciple echoes the master, except that even when Canseliet handles subtle intimations, as he generally does, he carefully controls his style and avoids the sudden clashing of too many images. Also inspired by the Golden Fleece, he offers some reflections on this theme in the wake of Fulcanelli.[157] More importantly, he devotes a whole study to the myth, published in 1936 and reedited several times.[158] Stating that he leaves aside those interpretations "adhering too strictly to history and mythology" (for him, this means euhemerism), he warns against a reading of this fable as a military venture subsequently adorned with fictional outgrowth and thus altered beyond recognition.[159] Dom Pernety had set out on the same crusade, only to substitute another form of reductionism for the historicizing mythographers. Canseliet's approach is more refined; for him, naturalistic alchemy always remains subservient to a philosophy. In this he is helped by the heuristics he has chosen for himself, namely philology—in the French sense of the term—a science which even when practiced unscientifically somehow offers, by its very nature, a safeguard. Indeed he does not call it "philology," but "kabbalistic phonetics," after Fulcanelli, meaning that figures and characters take on shape and substance, and play their roles together only through the medium of well-defined, well-chosen, happily combined words. In this, Canseliet belongs to the current earlier exemplified by many Jewish and Christian Kabbala writings, as well as by the bold speculations of a Fabre d'Olivet. But we must make clear from the outset that, although the principle of a symbolic phonetics appears valid in itself, with Canseliet this symbolism is often utterly fallacious. This author displays amazing combinations of ideas which are highly disputable.

Thus, it is "through the infallible medium of cabbalistic phonetics" that he intends to make a meaningful connection between the epic of the Argonauts and the processes of the Great Work. As a son of Aeolus, the god of wind, Athamas embodies here a primary agent, the wind, which our author illustrates with Plate 1 of Michael Maier's *Atalanta Fugiens,* where the picture itself is topped by the line "Portavit eum in ventre suo" from the *Emerald Tablet.* Athamas is also a name similar to Adamas, the primordial Adam (let us note, however, as Canseliet does not, that "Adamas" is not found in Hebrew). Of Nephelea, "symbolizing the original state, chaotic and nebulous, of the *subject of the sages,*" Ino takes the place, like some matter proceeding "toward the ultimate degree of perfection represented by the much-coveted fur." But "Nephelea" is also used to refer to a kind of *very subtle network, a net.* Her wild fit of madness provoked by Dionysus expresses volatility. Moreover, this character gives way to Ino, "who plays the role of mercury purified by sublimations." The aim of these operations is referred to by the corresponding Greek term, "Inao": "to empty," "to drain," "to purge." The daughter of Cadmus and Harmony, that is, of the black soil (cadmie) and the harmonic salt—in alchemy, the musical art—Ino gives birth to Learque, that is, *Lea* (stone) and *arkhê* (beginning, principle):Λέα, ἀφχη. The fruit of Nephelea's union with Athamas, "Phrixos reveals to us the aspect of the *philosophers' compost,* at the time of his birth." His name derives from "phrix": "shudder" or "ripple on a ruffled surface; flow, wave." Ino's sinful love for her son-in-law Phrixos prompts him to flee from her:

Similarly we can see, during the alchemical work, how the pure portion of the component separates from the putrefied mass, moves away from all danger and rises to the surface, carried up by a new substance of subtle complexion and similar to it as regards perfection. In this way does Hermes, in his *Tabula Smaragdina*, address the *son of science* and gives him some advice about how to operate: "Separate the earth from the fire and the subtle from the gross, softly and with great industry.[160]

Quite naturally, the ram Chrysomellos provides the symbol for such separation. Its name derives from Χφυδός "gold," and from μῆλον, "sheep" or "apple." Therefore, it means "golden apple," and recalls the fruit growing in the Garden of the Hesperides. As such, it is also the fruit of the love between Poseidon and a virgin named Theophany. And since this word means "apparition of the godhead in a human form," in an alchemical context we find mention of "the luminous and igneous emanation" of the godhead "within a corporeal and tangible body." Born to the god of the seas, Chrysomellos possesses an aqueous and mercurial nature; it is vitalized "by the universal spirit, whose luminous and stellar sign will appear before the artist's vision," as we can see in the *Speculum Veritatis'* second allegoric drawing, of which Canseliet gives a reproduction, and which is also featured in the present work (cf. figure VI). Let us look on this luminous skin as the star seen by the Magi, which shone brightly in the sky of Judea. Thus, Jason's trophy becomes the *Opus'* alpha and omega, symbolic here of both the matter worked upon and the 'medicine' state corresponding to the end of the operation.

Phrixos and Hellea's flight through the air upon the Ram "has to do with the operative phase resulting in the elixir (ϩοτγμ, sun: ιξις, arrival)" and in the discovery of "the sun hidden behind the star." The fall of the maid bears witness to the spiritual, igneous, and sulphurous aspects of this metal. While Hellea (Ελος, liquid plain, sea) does fall from the ram into the sea, similarly all the gross and adjustable elements disappear within the philosophers' *rebis,* which henceforth is free from the aqueous excess preventing its exaltation. Arriving in Colchis, Phrixos kills the ram, hangs his fleece on the branches of an oak, on the banks of the river Phasis (Φάσις, "showing, pointing to"; "vision," "appearance"). That is why Canseliet suggests that we look upon the oak as the initial raw and black mineral, and upon the Fleece as the operation's ultimate gem. Thus, the initial material becomes one with the final stone! And our author goes on to 'cabbalistically' relate the word "oak" ("*chêne*", pronounced [ken] in the dialect of northern France) to the Greek term Χην, *khên,* for "goose." The radical Χαινω,

Kaînô, means "opening," "opening up," or "gaping." It refers to the primordial chaos, for Χάος means: "jumble, obscurity, darkness, large opening, chasm." Hence "the nocturnal nativity, deep inside a cave, of the infant of Bethlehem."

Concerning Jason and his expedition, he remarks that the Ionian term Ιάζω, *Iazô,* means both "to speak Ionian," or "to chat" and "purple-colored," which directs our attention to the notion of the regenerated and glorious body said to be purple in color. Jason's name, then, would include the two colors that are farthest apart, that is red and blue—the former being the sublimation of mercury, the latter the sublimation of sulphur. But Canseliet (whose playing with phonetics is unfortunately wrong as regards philology) does not deal with the voyage of the Argonauts in Colchis, nor with their return, and he says he deliberately confined himself to the first part of the myth:

> Moreover, we would not have considered taking over Dom Antoine-Joseph Pernety's lengthy and detailed explanation given in his two scholarly volumes about the voyage of the ship *Argo.* The *humid* path followed by the Benedictine scholar, during this *hazardous navigation,* offers however some remarkable analogies with the *short path* so jealously guarded by the adepts and frequently concealed by them behind the former.[161]

He goes on to tell about the Knightly Order, and denounces as "ridiculous, if not dishonest" those who hold that this institution was supported by the handsome profits allegedly made by Philip the Good in the trading of wool. He thinks that the motto *"Aultre n'auray"* refers to the Virgin Mary, that the maxim *"Pretium laborum non vile"* teaches us that it is Chrysomellos' skin which, as a pendant, constitutes "the not-to-be-despised reward from the work." Canseliet's article contains many further elaborations, but most of them relate only indirectly to the Golden Fleece.

Fulcanelli's disciple has made two further references to this myth worthy of note. First, when studying the mansion of Le Plessis-Bourré, built around 1470 (cf. *supra*), the blazon beautifully represented on one panel in the hall with hermetic panelling (cf. our figure III) prompts him to make these comments:

> As true nobility would have it, Jean Bourré's armorial bearings arise here from the skin of the ram with the golden fleece, depicted here just after his conquest. The spirit of the world, its magnetism being attracted and held by the magic wool, is featured

once again, zigzagging on the field of the coat of arms. It is the same projection which falls from space and pervades the pieces of cloth spread in springtime by the couple of the *Silent Book* or Mutus Liber.[162]

Once again he sees a magnetism in the two fighting rams depicted on another panel nearby, which is also reproduced in his fine book. According to him, one of them is celestial, the other terrestrial, which expresses the play of a magnetism reminiscent of the *Emerald Tablet*'s line: "This is the power of all powers, for it will conquer everything subtle and penetrate everything solid." This means, our inspired commentator adds, the "struggle between the two spiritual currents presiding over the Great Work. Finally, Canseliet published a comprehensive study dealing with the motif of the Golden Fleece in the Palombara villa, which was built in the late seventeenth century.[163]

Perspectives

Ram, fleece, ship, book, Argonauts, and tomb are the landmarks in a scenario in which several hermetic figures take part. This is landscape, belonging to sacred geography and also bearing the marks of historical events, which engulfs the terrain of our discussion in the time of myth.

The ram appears to us to be the central image, the source of this symbology and its hermeneutics. A primal source from which spirit and matter arise, he is called *"medra"* or *"aja"* in Sanskrit, meaning "he who has no birth," and in contrast to Pisces' primitive ocean he appears as the driving force of the world, the manifestation of a creative ray of force. Associated with sun and fire, he acts as a mount for Agni, the creative god of the Hindus, while in Egypt, Ammon-Ra, the sun-god, wears the horns of this animal, which is associated with the cult of Osiris, for it is when exalted in this zodiacal sign that the sun feels night has been overcome. Chrysomallos, born from the condensation of a nebula, is the brother of the lamb of the *Revelation* (7.16), who opens the seven seals and is slaughtered as atonement. In John's text, this work is accomplished through the blood that colors the elects' white robes, just as Phrixos' hands become red with the blood of the animal. The fabled fleece was also white before Hermes covered or colored it with gold; he is a god who holds some secrets but is prepared to disclose them, just as Chrysomallos offers some advice to Phrixos, and Puss in Boots to his master.[164]

According to tradition, the noble metal is almost red and often associated with blood, so much so that the gradual shift in color corresponds with the process of the Great Work. Henceforth, there is an implicit but ever-present connection between the mystic lamb, the golden ram, alchemy, and—through the theme of the blood—the quest for the Grail, of which John the First of Portugal (in Van Eyck's polyptic in which mythical elements mix with historical figures) is at once a sponsor, a participant, and a new King Arthur.

Related to the theme of relinquishment and quest, we find also the *topos* of the skin. Pallas had a miraculous shield, an aegis (from the Greek word meaning "goat's skin"), covered with the skin of the goat Amalthea. The golden aegis is found in Homer, where we see Apollonios put it over Hector's dead body (*Iliad*, XXIV, 21), to make sure, it seems, that Hector's body would become incorruptible and his soul immortal. But the aegis is also a sign of terror or tumult, and so there is a distinction, in Greek, between goat skins and sheep skins. Casmilos, a youthful god, presides over their mysteries. The world of the souls and of the royal secrets, or of the shepherd-kings, is associated with the sheep and the rams rather than with the less peaceful goats. The sheep described by Apuleius (*Metamorphoses*, VI, 11–13) are frightening when driven by lust, but otherwise they bathe in the river peacefully; then Psyche, at Venus' command, can come and collect the tufts of their golden wool, which are stuck in the tangle of branches. This, strangely enough, is both suggestive of auriferous rivers and the traditional image of the golden bough.

Whether associated with gold or not, the woolen coat is an object of cult, Medea's for instance. This is because the animal's skin is thought to have a purifying, vivifying, creative quality, as evidenced by the myth of Orion: the ox's fleece has been fecundated by the sperm of the gods, or purified by their urine (symbolizing the evacuation of toxins, and therefore the rejection of passions). Here we come across a liquid connotation that may perhaps be related to the otter's skin—a water animal—on which the treasure of the Niebelungen lay. It is also on a marriage couch covered with the Golden Fleece, in a cave where sacred songs and dances are performed, that Jason and Medea unite. Described by Apollonios (IV, line 1140), the scene recalls the fine emblem in Michael Maier's *Atalanta Fugiens* (plate 23), where we see the Sun and Venus embracing each other in a shower of gold. Fecundation and rebirth through the skin—this is a well-known theme in ancient Egypt, where the sign "*mes*," representing three clustered skins, meant "to be born," or "to give birth."[165] And well before linen was used as a shroud, people went to heaven in a skin. Agni, according to Pausanias, used to wrap himself in such a skin. In the mysteries of Oropos, it was used as a device for inspiration, providing some light about the future and the other side of life. Sewn in this cradle-skin or vehicle-skin, King Dardanus crosses a chasm as if in the stomach of a fish; significantly, he is the father of one Jason, Cabir, or Dactyle, who is not unlike our Jason. The Hall of the Pythagorean basilica in Rome contains a fleece-shaped altar, symbolizing the threshold to be crossed by the candidate for initiation, and the tabernacle of Jahweh is fitted with a "blanket made of red-tinted ram skins."[166]

According to the prevalent alchemical notion, just as metals grown in the earth, similarly, and conversely, this skin so closely associated with the chrysopoeia can—according to both esoteric and popular, or Balzacian! belief—shrink when it wears off and no longer draws its energies from heaven. This is because, as the *Emerald Tablet* reminds us, the *Opus* is associated with the assistance of the sun and the moon. Even the Egyptians saw gold as a kind of magnet attracting, and refracting, sun rays upon obelisks and temples, or into the royal and funeral chambers (the latter contained amulets which symbolized indestructibility). Because of the dew which permeated the fleece of his ram during the night while the surrounding ground remained dry, Gideon became aware of his being God's chosen one (*Judges,* VI, 36-40). Similarly, as R. Roux notes in his beautiful book, the power hidden in the fleece of the Agrai rites became active in the sign of the Ram, in spring (in Athens it occurred in August). People thought that when such a skin was carried in procession, it absorbed the rays of Helios; young celebrants carrying three-plied fresh fleeces could then be seen climbing to the top of the Pelion.

The image of the lunar Nephele and of the sparkling coat is related to this symbolism of light. In the *Argonautica,* Medea and Jason see "the huge oak across which the fleece was hanging, like a cloud set aglow by the blazing rays of the rising sun.[167] This prefigures Jason's solar coat, which is described later in the same text as a "double coat of purple," a gift from Pallas, which shone so much that "it would have been easier to cast one's eyes upon the rising sun than behold the red glow of this coat; for red was the color of its background, while all its hems were purple."[168] This solar vestment, which has been likened to that of Demetrios Poliorcete representing the starry vault and the twelve signs of the Zodiac,[169] prefigures, of course, the one Jason wears:[169]

> Sometimes a maiden, when the full moon shines over her attic and collects its rays on the fine cloth of her robe, rejoices in her heart at the sight of its beautiful light: and Jason experienced the same joy when lifting the broad fleece in his hands; upon the fair complexion of his cheeks and forehead, the wool set a flame-like glow. The earth sent a vivid reflection of its glow before Jason's feet as he moved along. While walking, he sometimes put it over his left shoulder and let it hang loosely from the nape of his neck down to his feet; sometimes he rolled it up, touching it with both his hands, so afraid was he to be robbed of it by some man or god.[170]

   Although I have not seen it quoted explicitly, this beautiful passage
may have inspired some of our alchemists. It reminds us that the Fleece
can attract the moon to the earth,[171] and that Hermes himself presents
Nephelea, a figure of light, with the speaking ram: Hermes, a god who
likes thieves, who might well take back his gift, and who produced his
first lyre out of a cowskin. "Of Hermes and the ram in the Mother
mystery" Pausanias knew some esoteric functions, but he did not want
to disclose them; there is mention of a silver fleece covering the seat
upon which the Mother comes and sits to drink from the ritual cup, and
also of a stone clothed in wool, in Delphi, upon which the Mother-
Goddess is seated.[172] The god is also present on the ship Argo, where
several of his children can be found: Aithalides, of whom Pythagoras will
be a reincarnation, is the Argonauts' official herald, "the swift mes-
senger whom they entrusted with the embassies and the sceptre of
Hermes, his father, who had gifted him with an unfailing memory."
Aithalides' soul "sometimes roams among those dwelling in the underworld, sometimes comes back to broad daylight, among the living." Next
is Echion, whose name is suggestive of a snake. The third one, Erythos,
is associated with salvation—or resourcefulness. Hermes has also been
related to Jason, in light of ancient drawings.[173] And just as Athena has
inspired a thinking and talking ship, so also has Hermes produced, in his
image, a ram endowed with both these faculties, and then had it sacrificed. The corpse, while becoming a heavenly mystery, remained hanging on a tree, like Anubis whose sign is a skin hanging on a stake.[174] And
this stake, or tree, seems close enough to the standard: we need only
mention the living Agni, the standard of the gods, the standard of St.
Denys and of French chivalry.
   For the alchemists, however, the Golden Fleece is not a standard,
but a book. While in the *Revelation* to Jonn, the book with seven seals is
associated with the lamb, we have seen that in alchemical works the
Emerald Tablet sometimes tends to be identified with Chrysomallos'
skin, each supposedly bears sublime instructions and revelations. On
the strength of numerous examples, this is a comparison which can
eventually be taken for granted, but the link will perhaps appear more
obvious if we remember the scroll of the ancients, of those books rolling
and unrolling around one, or rather two, horns—therefore in a double
spiral, like the ram's horns.[175] And just as, covered with golden letters,
the tomb of Christian Rosencreuz (or of C.R.C) may, according to the
Rosicrucian *Fama*, be taken as a book encapsulating the whole
universe, so also can the Fleece, as we have seen, be used as a shroud
helping towards a new birth.
   In both cases, the condition of being wrapped up is experienced as

a journey, hence the frequent association with water, not only as water threatening to submerge the child-hero abandoned in the river, or as that water where Apuleius's sheep, with their golden wool, are bathing, but mostly as the ocean upon which Jason and his companions are sailing. Passing through water—or through air, like Phrixos—is often a prelude to ascending towards the sun, or a hint at a promised treasure, a glorious light, as we have seen in connection with the Gate of the Palombara villa.[176] Though Jason's ship and the Fleece cannot be interchanged, one aspect of them refers to the same initiatory theme: they are both a mythic object through which is accomplished a journey to some place where knowledge or a treasure can be secured. But by some natural shift in the symbolism, they came to signify in their own right this treasure or this knowledge. In Goethe's second *Faust*, almost contemporaneous with the sculpture of the Danish Thorwaldsen, we see nereids and tritons bringing the cabirs, which are dwarves—and so chthonian gods—from above. Now, the capturing of these cabirs is compared to the conquest of the Golden Fleece.[177] The object of the quest is identified with its vehicle, just as Argo, or the Fleece, can be seen alternately as carriers or carried objects. While going through Libya, the Argonauts take Argo on their backs, and also therefore the fabled skin which lies in the ship. Again, the connection between the Fleece and the Grail, suggested by the association of the ship and the fabled cup, seems quite significant: the Holy Vessel reminds us of Solomon's ship, met by Galaad and its two companions, and which contains the object of quest, just like Argo returned from Colchis. Argo, built with oaks sacred to Jupiter—and the alchemical AES, as we have seen, is sometimes associated with this god—plays the role both of a ferryboat and of a fabulous recipient.

It is on Chrysomallos that Phrixos goes to Colchis, and on Argo that Jason sets off to the same destination. A connection is also established between opposing or different 'orients', which refer to the configuration of a mythic or sacred space. For when the Ram and Phrixos part, the former becomes, in heaven, the king of the zodiac, and the latter, upon earth, a great king's son-in-law, as if, once the gods were appeased, disorder had given way to a restored order. But here is something even more unexpected: in the Phrixos episode, Colchis appears just as a Beyond beyond the seas, while the ram takes Helle in the air only to bring her to the ocean. Now, for some alchemists this Caucasian region was indeed nothing but the valley of tears, the land of the Fall. It would seem that a land of light had been deprived of its solar aspect and had become Saturnian. The Fleece was hanging from a tree, while the dragon mounted guard, just as in Paradise the tree of knowledge was standing with the serpent prowling about. Through some strange symbolic reversal, Eden is transformed here into a land of hard labor. A land, however, in which the Fleece hangs upon a tree and converts it into another tree of knowledge. (We note that the Greek μῆλον (*mêlon*) means both "apple" and "sheep.") Finally, Prometheus' blood is said to drop from a Caucasian mountain, and legend has it that the apostle Andrew went there to preach the Gospel. Colchis, a gateway to Caucasus, is therefore a land to be saved, a cardinal point in a spiritual space, of which Portugal, facing west, will explore the other direction.

For a long time, the Byzantines of the first millenium and down to the Middle Ages, subjected argonautic motifs and *topoi* mostly to euhemeristic readings, probably because mythic thought still found some fulfillment in organized religion, feeling no need to turn to ancient mythology for rejuvenation. Later on, the court of Burgundy provided a favorable milieu, out of which symbols blossomed forth into chivalrous and unexpected bowers. In Renaissance Italy, poets, artists, and humanists rode on Phrixos' mount, embarked on Argo, taking advantage of the fair wind exhaled by the fast rise of alchemy and the growing fascination for antiquity. With the Baroque, the Golden Fleece became germanized; in late German humanism, it branched out into inspired discourses, it became theosophized. Next came Pernety, who was marked by the style of the Enlightenment and probably given too much attention afterwards; he brought Argo to a standstill by the systematic use of monosemic allegory at the expense of metaphor, of metonymy, and of the plurality of meanings. But if, by nature, myths are endless, so too is their influence, just as a source of light can have its beams intercepted without becoming exhausted itself. In this way, in the twentieth century, two adepts' re-creative imagination was able to capture new lights radiating from the Fleece once gilded by Hermes. All this is perhaps an indication that inside Argo the doves are still awaiting their release and the exchange of signs to withdraw the ship from the Symplegades and the slimy bottom, to direct it towards ever new, ever similar, and endless routes.[178]

By means of its reservoir of motifs and themes, the myth of Jason and the Argonauts, with its connection to alchemy, sustains and denotes a chivalric imagery. Moreover, it gives to this imagery an opportunity to expand as it draws from a storehouse no longer limited to Christianity but also containing all the riches of paganism. When, in the age of Enlightment, three and a half centuries after the Burgundian innovation, chivalry had lost its active role—that is, its economic and military role—and turned into a storehouse of images, a mirror of symbols, it has become interiorized. As if etched out on the background of cultural and spiritual life, it stands now as a ship ready to accommodate new Argonauts or as some ram skin waiting for someone who can put it on and be restored to life. Freemasonry is the place for such possibilities.

The career of this fable of the Golden Fleece also reveals how myth and geography, as well as myth and history, are interrelated. It might, perhaps, prevent us from making a too rigid distinction between euhemeristic limitations and hermeneutic spaces, since we may find it more interesting to observe their interplay—as we have seen, the former are sometimes helpful to the latter. But it is indeed from the seventeenth century onward that such spaces unfold in a remarkable continuity of interpretation and notwithstanding the variety of forms they assume. Discontinuities appear even within this continuity, because behind the myth there is always room for fresh interpretations, for new symbolic realities. We may ask ourselves why the interpretation of Greek myths was so little diversified, and therefore not at all esoteric, until the late sixteenth century. Perhaps this is because two conditions had yet to be fulfilled. First, was the need for a well-established and varied *corpus* of images and myths, so that a range of possibilities could become available. Now, while the Renaissance had indeed contributed to such a corpus, it had not yet tapped into its symbolic possibilities in a spirit of creative freedom. Secondly, because this freedom had to be given the means for effective use: in society, by not being afraid of incurring the criticisms of established religions (although there was little to be feared from this quarter), and on a more individual level, by not being afraid to associate the truths of Christianity and the fables of paganism within the same discourse. Undoubtedly the basis of such association was already there in the sixteenth century, but it was not until the beginning of the next century that such inspired comparativism was to emerge, vivified by creative imagination, and so well-exemplified by the new readings of the myth of the Golden Fleece. At the same time we see the emergence of something that had been merely embryonic during the sixteenth, and even the late fifteenth century; that is, the coalescence of Alexandrian Hermetism, Kabbalah, and *Magia*: the very notion of esoteric tradition.

As in the days of Ficino or Pico, in fact, the 'concordance' work starting from the early seventeenth century consisted in binding together several cultural fields in the light of analogy, but now this stirring went on unrestrained, as never before. For there was indeed a multiplication of these fields: Christianity, music, poetry, emblematics, chemistry, etc. Hence a twofold necessity. First, the use of symbology with increasing flexibility, to make semantic passages and exchanges easier. Next, adoption of a heuristic code of reference, to give to this ever-extensible body a common basis, at least in theory. Now, it was the alchemical language and setting, taken as a departure point and a finishing point, which was chosen for this code. Thus alchemy in the seventeenth century, as a principle of (or a pretext for) comparativism, was the rope used for tying the sheaves gathered from various fields throughout the fifteenth century. From the late eighteenth century onward, alchemy was no longer necessary for this gathering, and in the nineteenth century the idea spread that this sheaf had always been there. The latter, actually, appears as a characteristic and auroral cluster, from whence emerged 'Tradition' as a selfexistent notion— which, in many areas and discourses of modern esotericism, it has fully become.

Appendices

**1) Michael Maier.—*Symbola Aureœ Mensœ duodecim Nationum*
—Frankfurt, 1617, p. 35. Cf. translation *supra*, page 25:**

"De Colchis Ammianus 1.22 narrat, *quod sint antiqua AEgyptiorum soboles, Diodorus eos AEgyptiorum* Colonias vocat, qui in Ponto habitant, fodinas metallorum secuti; Hinc aurea illa allegoria de *aureo* vellere Colchis asscripta est eam ob causam, quod illa regio metallis et illis mineris abundavit, quae ad Chemiae artem requiruntur: *Solis* filius in luco *Martis* pellem ouillam à *Mercurio* deauratam exposuit variis artificibus, quam tandem *Iason,* id est, medicus subtili stratagemate, ex *Medeœ,* hoc est, Rationis Theoreticae consilio, obtinuit: Primo *Draco* dentibus spoliandus erat (qui sunt materia artis purificata) per offam soporiferam, quae satis nota est herba colligenda sole ingrediente in capricornum, eum eo tempore radix eius sit maxime efficax: Secundo hi dentes in terram propriam spargendi sunt, quam terra Aquario sit subiecta, hoc est, aquosa vel aquas abundans: Tertio tauris terra subvertenda et supra semini spargenda: Hinc tumultus bellicus virorum mox crescentium et per se pereuntium, Atque hic est meta pellis aureae obtinendae."*

2) *ibid.,* pp. 586-588. Cf. *supra,* pages 25-26:

"non est, ait ille, cur timeas; Ego enim ut vivus nulli nocui, sed veluti *Medicus bonus* omnibus profui, sic nec vita defunctus, quamvis reuera mortuus non sim, sed fama, ut semper, vegetus & superstes: Hic soceri meri *AEetœ* regia sedes fugit, illi, Sol pater, non ille coelestis, quod absonum esset à ratione credere, sed longe alius, illi tamen nomine, facie & dignitate proximè compar. Hic in *Martis* nemore pellem Arietis à Mercurio deauratam suspendit, quam non absque magnis periculis obtinere mihi licuit, quemadmodum tu forte nouisti: Cui respondi, quantum lectione scire possum, non me fugit, at narra tute, quibus mediis ad eam rem veneris: Faciam, inquit ille, ut possum & promisi, sed ita, ut mentem potius intendas, quam aures, sensum potius, quam verba respicias, quo rerum cognitione magis, quam mole traditionum à me discedas: *Medea* mihi ut conciliatrix adfuit, sic ego tibi non deero. Illa ministrauit modum usurpandi stratagemata in obtinendo victoriam contra tot beluas veneno, flammis, dentibus nocentissimas: Eadem tibi quasi per manus reliquam, si dictis meis morigerus fueris: Draco pervigil sopitus mihi est massa narcotica in eius faces iniecta; Unde mox torpidus sensim caput in fundum dimisit semi mortuus. Cui ita iacenti exanimi absque morâ dentes extrahendi fuerunt. Hi mox in humum

propriam bobus ignivomis prius exaratam sepeliendi erant: Verum
boves indomiti, prius sub iugum mittendi; quod magnae industriae &
laboris fuit: Quocirca ad eos domandos aquam stillatitiam lympidissi-
mam dedit, in fauces illorum ad flammas resinguendas, inspergendam;
Praeterea *Lunae Solisque* imagines concessit, absque quibus nihil me
efficere posse ait: At ego, unde hæc omnia haberem, quaesivi? Satis tibi
dixi, respondit; Apud me enim non invenies, qui eas *Medea* ut accepi, sic
ipsa has secum abstulit: Ubi igitur investigem *Medeam,* refero? Hoc
incertum mihi, respondit. Postquam furibunda à me aufugit, nupta est
AEgeo seni, ex quo *Medum* filium peperit, cumque eo in Asiae regionem,
ab eo Mediam vocatam, abiit. His auditis plura alia ab eo percontari volui,
sed ille, defessus sum, inquit, interim hæc in mei memoriam serves;
quibus dictis evanuit. Ego vero cogitabundus super hac re diu manens,
quid significaret haec relatio, apud me meditatus sum, & post collat-
ionem omnium reperi, nil nisi *Medicinam* à me quæsitam subintelligi,
quae ex *Phœnice* revera petitur, at per vellus aureum adumbratur. Pili
enim animalis aurei & pennae volucris Phœnicis eodem spectant.
Doctos viros prætera, quos quærerem eadem de re hic paucos inveni,
quod tamen me parum movit, cum satis mihi fuerit, illam beatam
terram aeriam agnovisse: In hac enim mundi parte, inquam, *Syria est &
Terra Sancta.*"

Proposed translation:

*"There is no reason for you to be afraid. Since I have never done any
harm to anybody during my lifetime, but have been helpful to all as
a good physician, I did not die; I am still alive, full of life, in spite of
what people say. Here was the royal seat of my father-in-law AEtes,
son of the Sun—not the heavenly one, which would be an unreasonable belief, but of another of that name, much alike in appearance
and dignity. Here, in the field of Mars, he hung the skin gilded by
Mercury, which I could not get without great peril, as you probably
know."*

*I replied to Jason: "All that I may know as a result of my reading
has not slipped my mind, but tell me yourself how you managed to
do it."*

*He told me: "I shall do as best I can and as I promised, but I
request that your mind rather than your ears attend to me, that you
pay attention to the meaning rather than the words, in order that
through knowledge you learn more from me than from the mass of
traditions. Medea was beside me as a 'conciliator' just as I will now
extend my help to you. She indicated how, by making use of strata-*

gems, victory could be gained over so many hideous beasts, most harmful with their venom, flames, and teeth. I will pass these strata- gems on to you, as if from hand to hand, if you submissively mark my words. The awakened dragon was put to sleep by me through a dose of narcotics dropped into his throat; before long he was dozing and slowly drooped his head, as good as dead. From the beast lying there unconscious, the teeth had to be taken out without delay. These had to be quickly buried in a suitable soil, first ploughed by fire- spitting oxen, wild oxen that had been yoked previously. This could not be achieved without much toil and labor. That is why, in order to tame them, Medea provided drop after drop of a most clear water that was poured into their throats to extinguish the flames. Furthermore, she handed over to me the images of the Moon and the Sun, without which, she said, I would not get anywhere."

I asked Jason: "What about me? Where can I find all this?"

He replied: "I have told you enough. For it is not from me that you will get it. What I have received from Medea, she took away."

"Then, where can I find a trace of Medea?"

Jason replied: "I am not sure. After she left me, full of anger, she married old Aegea, whose son Medum she bore, and with him she set out for the region of Asia named after him and called Media.*"*

When I had heard all these things, I wanted to ask him something else, but he said: "I am tired. For the moment, take care of what I have just told you, in remembrance of me."

At this he vanished. And I, lost in throught, pondering for a long time over what I had heard, and bringing everything together, realized it was the medicine *I was looking for, that which is indeed expected from the Phoenix, but which is represented by the Golden Fleece. For the hair of the golden creature and the feathers of the Phoenix both refer to the same thing. Afterwards I found in this place only a few learned men whom I could question on this matter; anyway I was no longer really interested, because for me it was enough to have been acquainted with this blessed aerial land. Indeed, it is in this part of the world that Syria and the Holy Land lie.*

3) Jacques (Clovis Hesteau) de Nuysement. *Traittez du vray Sel secret des Philosophes et de l'Esprit général du monde.* Paris, 1621, pages 295-301. Cf. *supra*, pages 28-29:

"Come entre les autres celle de Jason et Médée, selon le tesmoi- gnage de Suídas élégamment rapporté Crisogone Polidore en sa préface sur les œuvres de Geber. En faveur de laquelle je me dispenseray du silence promis, pour déclarer que ce nom de Médée veut dire cogitation,

méditation, ou investigation; tirant sa dérivation d'un mot qui signifie
Principe, Origine, source, ou raison. Car toute méditation, cogitation, ou
investigation, doit sans doute avoir quelque principe ou raison pour
fondement sur qui elle soit apuyée, et d'où elle sorte: Iuy donnant
occasion de faire telle recherche avec ratiocination. Cette Médée apprit
à Jason (qui est l'inquisiteur ou Philosophe) deux choses ausquelles
consiste toute la Philosophie. La première est de conquester la toison
d'or, qui est l'art destiné aux transmutations métalliques avec les choses
minéralles. La seconde est la restauration des corps débilitez par
maladies; en les guarissant promptement et parfaitement: puis leur
restituant cette jeunesse ou première vigueur allentie, et presque
esteinte par le froid aconit des ans. Chassant des corps par cette
médecine uniquement universelle, toutes humeurs et superfluitez
corrompues et corrompantes qui les conduisent à leur fin, le plus
souvent précipitée par l'excès de tels accidents impréveus. Ces deux
miraculeux effects furent atteints et accomplis par Jason, observant
religieusement les utiles conseils de la sage Médée: après toutefois une
longue et laborieuse navigation suivie d'infinis périlleux hazards, à
cause du dragon et des Taureaux qu'il luy convient dompter. Or cette
navigation est la pénible recherche et douteuse expérience des choses,
où l'on vogue souvent tout le temps de la vie sans pouvoir arriver au port
de cette immense mer de la Nature. Ces Taureaux monstrueux qu'il faut
assujettir et accoupler au joug, sont les fourneaux où se doivent faire les
opérations; lesquels représentent naïvement la teste d'un Taureau, et
jettent le feu par les yeux et la gorge, ainsi que dit la fable. Car il est
nécessaire qu'il y ait des souspiraux par lesquels soient reiglez les
degrez de la chaleur, et le feu préservé d'estouffement, d'autant que si
l'on n'est maistre du feu il arivera beaucoup d'accidents pendant le
cours de l'oeuvre, qui frauderoit l'ouvrier de son attente. J'en puis parler
comme expert: car de neuf vaisseaux que je mis en décoction pour
trouver le vray degré de chaleur, leshuit périrent; et ne me resta que
celuy par le moyen duquel furent faites les expériences dont j'ay cy
devant parlé. Ce dragon toujours veillant est ce Mercure général que
Cadmus sceut autrefois tuer, c'est à dire fixer. Le champ de Mars où il
falloit semer les dents du serpent martial, n'est autre chose que le
vaisseau dans lequel s'esleuent ces soldats armez de lances aigües.
Lequel vaisseau ne doit point estre en cet endroit un allembic de verre
comme pense et dit Pollidore. Mais une forme de Cabacet ainsi que dit la
fable, estroit en bas et s'eslargissant fort par le haut. Et faut qu'il soit de
bonne terre bien cuite: et non de fer ou de verre. Au fond duquel
s'esleuera un camp armé et hérissé de lances, qui semblent horrible-
ment irritées, se coucher l'une contre l'autre pour combattre ainsi

qu'en plain champ de bataille. Voilà ce qu'a ingénieusement inventé le Poëte, pour fair admirer au vulgaire come fort estrange et inouïe, une chose tellement familière, que si je la nommois on se moqueroit de luy et de moy. Mais après que Jason eut accomply ses labeurs, il luy fallut encore endormir le dragon veillant qui gardoit la Toison d'Or; et l'assoupir de sorte que de son gosier ne sortist plus ni feu ni fumée. Ce qu'il feit, en le noyant dans les eaux Stigiennes: c'est à dire, en le redissolvant et refixant avec son esprit. Il ne restoit donc plus à Jason pour posséder la Toison d'Or, et rajeunir son père Æson agravé de vieillesse extresme, sinon un seul labeur que Médée luy enseigna pour couronner ses bons offices; c'estoit la fermentation et conjonction du beurre du Soleil avec la paste de ce Mercure préparé; qui de soy n'est capable de produire deux si excellents effects: n'estant à vray dire, que la terre où l'on doit semer le pur froment que Nature a produit et conduit à la perfection qui luy est concédée. Par ce dernier labeur il se veid enfin maistre de ce double trésor, qu'il emporta glorieusement au lieu de sa naissance: avec lequel il se combla de ses richesses, et son vieil père de vigoureuse santé; banissant de luy les importunes langueurs que traisne après soy le long âge. Je laisseray donc maintenant Jason et sa Médée jouir de leur félicité, et diray seulement que rien ne pourroit estre exprimé par ce dragon veillant et jettant le feu par la gorge, plus proprement que nostre esprit ou Mercure, qui est la chose du monde la plus vive et inflammable".

Nuysement's work ends with: *Sonnet. En conclusion de ce livre* (cf. also the edition provided by Sylvain Matton, *supra*, note 65):

> Qui cherche donc l'honneur, la gloire, et l'heur du monde,
> Soit Philosophe, artiste, et il en joüira;
> Car la Philosophie en fin le conduira
> Au sommet des tresors dont la Nature abonde.
> De luy la nuit d'erreur où vainement se fonde
> L'aveugle opinion elle dissipera,
> Et de la vérité le jour esclaircira,
> La tirant hors du sein de la machine ronde.
> Quand Jason eut conquis ce bien tant désiré,
> Qui par l'experiment le rendit asseuré
> De vivre riche et sain plus qu'il n'eust osé croire,
> Desdaignant la misère, et bravant le trespas,
> Egal aux demi-dieux ne possedoit-il pas
> Du monde universel l'heur, l'honneur, et la gloire?

Proposed translation:
And, among others, that of Jason and Medea, according to Suidas'

account, finely reported by Crisogone Polidore in his preface to Geber's works. In favor of which I shall depart from the promised silence, in order to state that the name "Medea" means "cogitation, meditation, or investigation," deriving from a word meaning "principle, origin, source, or reason." For all meditation, cogitation, or investigation must have some underlying principle or reason upon which it is based and from which it arises, giving the opportunity for thoughtful research. This Medea taught Jason (who is the inquisitor or philosopher) two things making up the whole philosophy. First, how to conquer the Golden Fleece, which is the art which aims to transmute metals with minerals. Second, how to restore bodies weakened by diseases, through quick and perfect healing, then through restoring them to their youth or primal vigor, diminished and almost extinct due to the passing of years; and removing from bodies, through this unique and universal medicine, all corrupted and corrupting humors and superfluous matters which bring about their end, usually hastened by unexpected accidents. Both these miraculous effects were achieved and accomplished by Jason, religiously following the helpful advice of the wise Medea; this, however, after a long and laborious navigation followed by endless perilous hazards, because of the dragon and the bulls he had to tame. Now, this navigation is the difficult search for and doubtful experience of things, where we often drift along during our whole lifetime, unable to reach the port of this huge sea of Nature. These monstrous bulls which have to be yoked together are the furnaces where the operations must take place; these naively represent the head of a bull, and send out fire through their eyes and throats, as told in the fable. There must be some openings at the base, through which the degree of heat may be regulated and the fire prevented from choking; also if fire is not under our control, many accidents will happen during the course of the work, deceiving the worker's expectations. I am one who can speak about this as an expert: for out of nine vessels into which I put a decoction to find out the right degree of heat, eight were destroyed; and I was left only with that one through which the experiments I have related so far were conducted. This ever-watchful dragon is Mercury, which Cadmus, in the past, was able to kill, that is, to fix. The field of Mars, where the teeth of the martial serpent had to be sown, is nothing other than the vessel in which these soldiers arise armed with sharp spears. That vessel is not to be taken here as a glass still, as Pollidorus thinks and says, but as a kind of "cabacet," as the fable says, narrow at the bottom and opening out towards the top. And it must be of good, well-baked earth, not of iron or glass. From its bottom will spring up an armed camp, bristling with spears looking terribly irritated, lying one against the other to fight as if in the midst of the battlefield. Such is the ingenious invention of the Poet, to have the common folk admire as a very strange and unheard-of thing, one so familiar that if I were to name it, he and I would make ourselves a laughingstock. But after he had accomplished his works, Jason had yet to put to sleep the dragon watching over the Golden Fleece; and to do it in such a way that neither flame nor smoke would come out from his throat. This he achieved by drowning him in the Stygian waters: that is by re-dissolving and re-fixing him with his spirit. So, to possess the Golden Fleece and restore to youth his father AEson, afflicted with extreme old age, Jason had only one more labor to do, which Medea taught him as the culmination of her good offices. This was the fermentation and conjunction of the Sun butter with the paste of this prepared Mercury, which by itself cannot produce two such excellent effects, being in truth nothing but the soil where the pure wheat must be sown which Nature has produced and brought to the perfection it is meant to achieve. Through this final labor, he at last found himself the master of this twofold treasure, which he gloriously brought to his birthplace: he showered himself with its riches and bestowed his old father with robust health, chasing away from him the troublesome languidness which old age trails in its wake. Now then, I shall let Jason and his Medea enjoy their bliss and only say that nothing could be more appropriately expressed by this watching, fire-belching dragon than our spirit of Mercury, which is the quickest and most inflammable thing in the world. [...]

> *He, then, who seeks honor, glory and worldly happiness,*
> *Let him be a philosopher, an artist; he will derive joy*
> *therefrom;*
> *For in the end philosophy will take him*
> *To the greatest treasures found aplenty in Nature.*
> *The darkness of delusion, whereupon in vain*
> *Blind opinion rests, it will remove from him,*
> *And with truth will brighten the day,*
> *Drawing it out of the womb of the round machine.*
> *When Jason had conquered this much-desired good,*
> *The experience of which insured*
> *That he enjoyed wealth and health in his life*
> *Beyond all expectations,*
> *Ignoring misery and braving death,*

On a par with the demi-gods, was he not in possession
Of the universal world's happiness, honor, and glory?

4) Johann Valentin Andreae. *Chymische Hochzeit: Christiani Rosencreütz. Anno 1459.* **Strasbourg, 1616. Cf. translation** *supra,* **page 27:**

"Nach dem wir uns nuhn erstlich aus dem Brunnen gewaschen,
auch jeder ein Trunck auss einer gantz guldin Schalen gethan: Musten
wir der Jungfrawen noch einmal in den Sall folgen und daselbsten newe
Kleyder anziehen: Diss waren gantz guldine Stuck, mit Blumen herrlich
gezieret. So wurde auch jedem ein ander Guldin Flüss gegeben, welche
mit Edelgestein ubersetzt waren and mancherly wirckung nach jedes
wirckhener Krafft mit sich bracht. Daran hieng ein schweres stuck
Gold, darauff waren Sonn und Mond gegen einander gebildet, auff der
andern seiten aber stund dieser Spruch: dess Monds Schein wirt sein
der Sonnen Schein, und der Sonnen Schein wirt siebenmal heller sein,
dann jetzt."

5) Johannes de Monte Hermetis. *Explicatio Centri in Trigono Centri
per Somnium.* **Ulm, 1680. Cf. translation** *supra,* **pages 29-30:**
"Ohne Zweifel wird dir bekandt seyn die Histori von dem alten
Heidnischen rittermässigen Helden Jasone welcher auss Trieb seines
tapferen Gemüths das erlange wolte, was zu seiner Zeit allen andern zu
erlangen unmüglich; Nemlich den in Griechenland Hochberühmten, in
einer weit entlegenen Insul Cadmo aber enthaltenen, hochschätzbarten
Güldnen Fluss; dieweilen er dann solches so wohl mit Versöhnung
seiner Götter, als auch mit gutem Vorbedacht und Einrathen verstä-
ndiger Leute, welche in selbiger Insul wohneten, für die Hand nahme,
als ist ihm wol gelungen und hat den überaus grossen Schatz dess
gedachten Güldenen Fluss mit Heldenmässiger Hand druch grosse
Mühe und Arbeit davon getragen. / Wann mir dann wohl wissend, dass
noch heutigen Tags solche rittermässige Helden, welche sich in
Bestreitung dess Hermetischen Güldenen Fluss wol gebrauchen lies-
sen, möchten gefunden werden, wo ihnen nur einige Mittel selbigen zu
erlangen, an die Hand geben würden, als hab ich mich dess gemeinen
Vers erinnern wollen: *scire tuum nihil est, nisi te scire hoc sciat
alter.*"

6) Ehrd de Naxagoras. *Aureum Vellus Oder Güldenes Vliess.* **Frankfurt, 1733, t. I, pp. 37-39 et 80. Cf.** *supra,* **page 37:**
"Vellus Aureum dahero aber eighentlich und recht Teutsch: Eine
goldene Wolle, so auf der Welt kein andere, als alleine der Weisen ihr

bekannter Widder trägt, das ist der in aller Welt, obschon unbekannte, dennoch beruffene Lapis Philosophorum ist, weil er von solchem Widder herkommet, in welchem die Philosophische Sonne ihre Exalation hat, oder in ihren Horizont streichet, denn gedachter Widder noch nicht der Lapis Philosophorum selbst, sondern nur desselben Materie ist, aus welcher er zuförderst noch extrahirt ausgezogen, oder abgebrochen werden muss, und also ein von seiner Form abgeschiedenes Centrum, so alle drey Principia Naturæ et Artis gleichwohl noch in sich, aber aufs allerhöchste gereiniget und geistlich gemacht hat, oder eigentlicher ein aus seinem Centro, durch die Kunst heraus gerissener Metallischer Saame, das wahre Sperma oder Prima Materia Lapidis Philosophorum ut & omnium metallorum, so ein leichtflüssiges Gold, das in alle Metallen wei Œhl in Leder eingeht; Welches nächst Gott, aller wahren Philosophorum Anherr oder Vater der grosse König und Philosophus Hermes Trismegistus welchen Nahmen er daher hat, weil er nicht alleine alles das, so in der Welt ist, und nur eine Materiam oder Form hat, und also aus den 4. Elementen zusammen gesetzt worden, davon denn unzehlich viele Theile in der Welt seyn, in drey fürnehmliche Theile, als in partem Animalem, Vegetabilem et Mineralem, von welchen allen und jeden er insonderheit für allen andern Philosophis sonderlichen gründlichen Verstand gehabt, sondern auch diese tres Partes Philosophiæ in dem NB. unico lapide benedicto begriffen, und seines Gefallens damit NB. in Opere Solis gehandelt hat, sein Superius ac Inferius nennet, welches aus dem weissen Widder ausgezogen werden muss, wie er denn auch auf seiner Smaragdenen Taffel, worauf die Kunst vollständig beschrieben, expressè setzt: Du solst das Erdreich scheiden vom Feuer und das subtile von dicken, kurtz, es liegt Ignis & Azoth, welche die Philosoph: alleine als ein Sperma virile & muliebre zum Wercke gebrauchen, und nicht mehr in solchem einigem Dinge verborgen, welches sie also hoch und tieff in so wunderliche Reden und Nahmen verstecket, darinnen verborgen.

Welchem allen nicht zuwider ist, dass Ovidius in seinem 7ten Buche und erstem Gedichte der Verwandelung, solches bald ein goldenes Lamm oder Widder, bald ein goldenes Fell bald eine goldene Wolle oder Fluss, oder Vliess nennet, denn mit dem Lamme oder Widder zeiget er bloss dasjenige an, welches die goldene Wolle träget oder das Subjectum Philosopiæ, mit dem Fell aber, worauf die Kunst beschrieben gewesen. Und dass ich es recht Teutsch und aufrichtig vor Gott und aller Welt sage, so ist in Colcho das Fell, welches man abusivè, den Widder oder auch Aureum Vellus schon selbst nennet, eben das was Hermetis Smaragdene Tafel gewesen, ratione dessen, weil auf des letztern die gantze Kunst kurtz und gut beschrieben gewesen, und weil nicht alle

und jede diese Tafel haben können, also ist nöthig gewesen, dass die
andern solches abgeschrieben und ist also kein anderer Unterschied
darunter, als das eine auf einen kostbahren Smaragd, welcher es zur
selbigen Zeit genug auch in Grosso durch die Kunst gemacht gehabt, als
die Historici beglauben das andere aber auf einen blossen Pergament
beschrieben gestanden, im übrigen ist es einerley). Unterdessen bleibt
solche Abschrift, ob sie schon auf schlechtem Pergament beschriben
war, sowohl als die Smaragdene Tafel nur in der Königen und Priester
Händen, welche letztere die Kunst zum Theil auch verstunden, weil sie
gemeiniglich in denen ein oder andern Heydnischen Gott geweyheten
Tempeln aufbehalten worden, wie man denn auch bey den alten His-
toricis liesst, dass gemeiniglich die Priester zu ihren Königen erwahlet
worden, oder zum wenigsten kein anderer darzu, welcher die Kunst
nicht verstanden, auf dass sie nicht Ursache hätten, auf denen armen
Unterthanen immer als wie ein Adler auf einem Aase zu liegen und ihnen ihr Blut auszusaugen, ja die Könige selbsten haben vermeynet, dass
sie anders nicht wohl regieren könnten, wo sie nicht der Egyptier
Künste verstünden, welche waren die Theologia (ob schon nach ihrer
Art), die Astronomia und die Hermetische Philosophie oder Alchymia
[. . . .p. 80:] Smaragdene Tafel und Pergament haben beyde das
Fundament und gantze Procedur der Kunst vollkommen beschrieben,
in sich gehalten, als wie auf den zwey Taffeln Mosis, in Gleichnüss, die
zehen Gebothe Gottes enthalten, und auf den 7. steinern Taffeln, in
vorhergehendem gedacht, die 7. freye künste".

Proposed translation:

So in German "Vellus Aureum" *means literally* "a golden wool," *the
like of which cannot be found in the world, except that worn by the
ram well-known to the sages. This wool is the* Lapis Philosophorum,
*unknown in the whole world although renowned: it comes from the
ram, wherein the philosophic sun finds its exaltation, or rather it
passes over the horizon of that sun. Indeed, our ram is not yet the*
Lapis Philosophorum *itself, but only the matter of this stone. Conse-
quently, we should also extract this stone or break the matter to get it.
The Fleece, therefore, is a* Centrum *separate from its form; it still contains within itself the three principles of nature and the art, but extremely purified and spiritualized. Or rather, it is a metal seed
pulled from its center by the art. This is the real sperm or prime
material of the philosophers' stone and of all metals; this is a light
and liquid gold which pervades all metals as oil pervades leather.
Next to God, the father or ancestor of all true Philosophers, is the great*

king and philosopher Hermes Trismegistus, named after this: all there is in the world is of one matter or form only and was made out of the four elements, the innumerable parts of which are divided into three kingdoms: the animal, the vegetable, the mineral. Hermes Trismegistus, in order that everyone, and especially other philosophers, could understand perfectly, has made this distinction and shown how these parts of philosophy are included in one and the same blessed stone (with which he was pleased to deal in De Opere Solis*) which he calls* "Superius ac Inferius." *That is what should be extracted from the white ram. About this also he tells explicitly in his* Emerald Tablet, *where the art has been described in full: "Thou shalt separate earth from fire and the subtle from the dense." In short, there is fire and azoth, which the philosophers alone are using in their work, as a male and female sperm. The latter is no longer hidden within the single thing which the philosophers conceal in the depths and peculiarities of their discourses and of the names they use.*

This is not in conflict with Ovid's mentioning, in his seventh book, in the first poem of the Metamorphoses, *somethimes a golden lamb or ram, sometimes a golden skin, sometimes a golden wool or river, or again a fleece. By "lamb" or "ram" he simply refers to that which acts as a support for the golden wool, a support which is the* Subjectum Philosophiæ, *while the skin is that upon which the art is written. And to tell it in truth and in good German before God and before the world: in Colchis the skin improperly called ram or even* aureum vellus *is nothing else but that which was Hermes' Emerald Tablet, for the reason that upon this tablet the whole art has been well described in summary. And since not everyone is able to get this tablet, it has been necessary that others write this text. So there is no difference between both texts, other than one has been written upon a precious emerald made at the same time through alchemic art—as historians believe—while the other has been written on a mere piece of parchment. But basically, this is the same thing. As a matter of fact, this copy, although made on poor parchment, remained, just like the Emerald Tablet, only in the hands of kings and princes who understood the art at least partially, as a result of their having lived generally for some time in either of the pagan temples dedicated to God. Moreover we can read in the ancient historians that it was the priests who, usually, were chosen as kings—or at least only those men who could understand the art—so that they found no reason to prey upon the poor subjects like eagles upon carrion, or to suck their blood. And the kings themselves maintained that they could not rule*

properly without understanding the arts of the Egyptians, namely
theology (although in their own way), astronomy, and hermetic
philosophy or alchemy [. . .] So both texts contain the foundation
and the complete process of the art, perfectly described, just as Moses'
two tablets contain the symbol of the ten Commandments of God, and
as the seven liberal arts are found on seven stone tablets.

7) *Ibid.*, p. 66. Cf. *supra*, pages 37-38:
    "Absonderlich ist Democritus, ein Mann von einem sehr hohen
Verstande, dahero geursachet worden, sich auch in Egypten zu begeben,
der Natur Geheimnüsse und die wahre Philosophiam daselbst zu erler-
nen, wie er denn auch deswegen des Egyptischen Priesters Dardani
Grab heimlich eröffnet, und die Bücher so bey ihme gelegen, und darinnen die goldene Philosophie oder verborgene Geheimnüsse der
Natur, id est, das Aureum Vellus, beschrieben gewesen, daraus genom-
men, und mit sich in Griechen-Land geführet, darinnen studiret und
letzlich selbst Bücher von der Alchymia geschrieben und hinterlassen,
als Tincturam Auri, Argenti et Lapidum."

8) *Ibid.*, p. 82. Cf. *supra*, page 38:
    "Das Vitrum ist eins deren Dinge, wodurch die Præparation
befördert wird, denn durch die Reduction des Eisens zur Natur des Vitri
præparati werden viele Irdigkeiten abgeschieden das übrige zu über-
gehn, weil des gesagten allen verborgenen Verstand doch keiner so
leichte ohne einen treuen Lehrmeister ergründen wird. Dahero denn
auch Hermes nicht ohne Ursache die Kunst auf einen Smaragd nicht
sehr ungleich einen schönen blauen Saphier, in Grösse einer Tafel
beschrieben, sondern vielmehr dadurch anzuzeigen, dass auch die
gantze Kunst auf dergleichen grüne oder Saphir-Farbe gegründ, wovon
das erstere bey dem Hermete und das andere bey dem Prophet Esaia zu
lesen, sonderlich bey dem erstern, da auch auf der Tafel steht: Und wie
alle Dinge von einem kommen der es bedacht hat, also kommen und
entspriessen auch alle Dinge (so zur Kunst gehören) aus dem Dinge
das da vereiniget die würdigsten Theile durch einen Weg und Diposition,
wie denn die wahren Philosophi auch einhellig warnen, dass man nichts
frembdes darzu bringen solle."

9) *Ibid.*, pp. 49 s. Cf. *supra*, pages 39-40:
    "[. . .] nach langer und gefährlicher Schiffung auf dem Philo-
sophischen Meer, das ist, in Studirung und Lesung der Philosophorum
Schrifften, als welche wohl gleichsam nichts anders als ein recht un-
ergründliches wüstes wildes Meer, worauf sich keiner vorfinden wird,

er habe dann einen richtigen Compass bey sich, welcher der eintzige Verstand der Concordanz ist, weil sie unzehlichen Gefahren wegen derselben Drachen, Löwen und andern ungeheuren Thieren unterworffen. Diese Schiffung nun ist die fleissige Nachforschung und die zweifelhafftige Erfahrung der Dinge so zur Kunst gehören, und derselben Præparation, in welchen beyden offtmahls derer viele die meiste Zeit ihres Lebens zubringen, und doch nicht in dem gewünschten Port des grossen Meers der Natur anlanden können.

Und ist diss füwahr eine sinnreiche Poetische Erfindung, auch die Kunst einigermassen unter der Historie selbsten Leuten die Sache wunderlich macht, als was frembdes und unerhörtes, welches uns doch sehr gemein und bekannt ist, dass so ich es benenen würde, man ein Gelächter dräüber anzustellen, Ursache hätte, NB. concordirt also in diesem Stücke mit Henrico Madatano oder Hadriano von Mynsicht, alsbald auch folgen wird, wiewohl in meiner allerunterthänigsten Dedication bereits schon dessen gedacht worden."

10) Hermann Fictuld. *Aureum Vellus Oder Goldenes Vlies.* **Frankfurt, 1749, pp. 169–170. Cf.** *supra,* **page 42:**

"[Nephele] gab ihnen in Verwahrung dasjenige goldene Buch oder Rollen, die vermutlichen, nach damahligen Gebrauch von Schaaf- oder Lammes-Fällen zusammen gestoppet und eine lange Rolle darvon gemacht, und, wie noch heut zu Tage unter den Juden dass Mosaische Gesetz, die Propheten und Psalmen geschrieben werden, darauf, nach der alten Weise, mit Ziffern, Characteren, Littern, Figuren und Bildern von Gold, die hohe Kunst und Wissenchaft der Alt-Väter signiret und bezeichnet war; und zwar nicht allein die Gold-Erzeugungs-Kunst, sondern zugleich alle sieben Wissenschaften der hohen Weissheit, der Magie, Cabalæ und Astronomie [. . .] die als eine Testamentliche Gabe in dem Königlichen Cabinet verwahret lage, solten nehmen, und darmit entweder in ein abgelegene Wüsten und Land, oder aber, zu ihren Vettern, der Mutter Bruder, dem König in Colchis, in Georgien, Migrelien, heut zu Tag Odisey genannt, welcher Ort von ihnen jenseits über dem schwartzen Meer gelegen, als ihren vormahligen Vaterlande, fliehen und ziehen solten; allwo sie sichern und vergnügten Auffenthalt finden, leben, und sich erhalten könten."

11) *Ibid.,* **pp. 307–312. Cf.** *supra,* **pages 43–45:**

"Die Sonne, Athamas, der feurige solarische Sulphur, ist der Vater dieses edlen Kindes. Denn von der Sonne, dem Athamas, fliesset heraus der feurige martialische Samen, das edle Feuer-Leben, die Tinctura Solis, der Spiritus Tingens, der Astral-Geist der obern Elemente und

Ausflüsse, welche da sich in seine Matricem und Behältnisse der
unterirdischen Regionen herabsencken, durch den Mond, die Nephelen, der wässerigen lunarischen Ausgüsse, u. der Leidenschafften, in
seine Mutter; Denn vom Monde fliesset heraus der wässerige, aber sehr
feurige venerische Samen des sanfften Liebes-Feuer-Lebens, der weise
Lunarische Mercurius, der Samen des Weibes, der astralische weise
Geist, das weise Wasser, das trockene, die Hände nicht nass machende,
Wasser, das grosse Solvens, der Weisen Alcahest, in welchem das Gold
der Weisen Radicaliter solviret und flüchtig gemacht wird, das da sonst
kein ander Ding in der Welt vermag. Als wolte Hermes sagen, ihr solt
wissen, dass die Sonne ein grosser und mächtiger Planet am Grayss des
Himmels, und, nach der astronomischen Ausrechung 140. mahl
grösser denn der Erd Globus, darzu einer gantz feurigen Eigenschafft
ist, gleich als ob es ein grosses Meer voll geschmoltzen Metall wäre, die
da ihre Strahlen ausgiesset, als ein im Fluss auf dem Test stehendes
Gold: so, dass wenn deren Strahlen sich gerade herunter nach der
Erden sencken solten, so müste alles zu Staub und Asche verbrennen;
Allein der liebe Gott hat nichts erschaffen, das zum Verderben dienet,
sondern er hat es alles weisslich und gut gemacht, wie er denn diesen
grossen Planeten erschaffen zur Erwärmung der kalten feuchten
Erden, der kalten Mercurialischen Theile, so hat er doch derselbigen
entgegen gesetzt den kalten Mond, einen kalten feuchten Planeten, der
da als ein dritter Mann, so zwischen der Sonnen und der Erden
schwebet, und 42 mahl kleiner ist, denn der Erd-Globus, in welchem
sich die feurigen Strahlen der Sonnen concentriren und ablöschen,
und welcher alsdenn, wenn sie gemildert sind, sothanen eingeflössten
und impægnirten Samen wieder der Erden zusendet; so, dass Athamas
und Nephelen, durch ihr königliches Ehe-Band, zwey königliche
Kinder, Phrixus und Höllen, das ist, einen solarischen Sulphur und
lunarischen Mercurius, gebohren in dem königreiche Theben, der
obern Elementen und Regionen, die allda nicht bleiben konten,
sondern musten herab, und aus ihres Vaters Königreiche und Mon-
archie verjaget werden. Denn Nephelen, der Mond, die Mutter, war,
wegen geringer oder schwacher Constitution und allzu grosser Kälte,
nicht vermögend die Samen und Ausgeburten der Sonne zu behalten,
sondern muste sich selbiger entziehen, als ob sie gestorben, da denn das
übrige Gestirne, und sonderlich der Jupiter seine widrige Gemüths-
Affecten, gleich denen Stieff-Müttern und Priester-Rotte, als einen
arsenicalischen Mercurium und Sulphur einfliessen lassen, und
dadurch zu wege brachten, dass diese Kinder ihre obere Region
verlassen, und, als in einem gesegneten Regen, mit dem goldenen Vlies,
dem grossen goldenen Widder, durch die Lufft-Region herab in die

aetherische irdische Kälte, auf die Erden fahren musten, und in deren Principien und Elementen, als in dem Königreiche Colchis, sind sie herrlich aufgenommen worden.

Ino, die Seite-Gemahlin des Athamas, bedeutete die widrigen Aspecten und Impressiones des Gestirns, die da vom Jupiter ihren Ursprung haben, Jupiter aber ist ein Patron des Priester-Geschlechts. Daher wird gesagt, dass Ino, als eines Priesters Tochter, zwar denen zwey Kindern sehr erträglich und vortheilhafftig gewesen wäre, so die doch aber von Anfange der Dinge nicht war, sondern erst nach dem Fall Lucifers und Adams, durch den von Gott ausgesprochenen schrecklichen Fluch, als eine Neben-Sache geurständet, eingeschlichen und eingedrungen sey: das ist, die Arsenicalischen Geister, die widrigen Impressiones sind als eine zweyte Ehe anzusehen, und als eine Stieff-Mutter zu betrachten: Und zwar darum, wie bekannt, dass alles, was vom Priesterlichen Stande und Stamm herkommt oder gebohren wird, von einer besonderen Art, bosshafft, verkehrt, verächtlich, verschmitzt, heuchlerisch und lügenhafft, je hochtrabend und stoltz ist. Wie denn der liebe Heyland Christus Jesus selbst darüber klaget, wenn er saget, und gar öffters wiederholet: Wehe euch, ihr Pharisäer und Schrifftgelehrten, ihr Heuchler, ihr Schlangen, ihr Ottergezüchte, wie wolt ihr der höllischen Verdammniss entrinnen. Matth. 23. Dahero auch die Stieff-Mutter in einem besondern ausnehmenden bösen Credit stehen, der ihnen in der gantzen Welt nachgehet, dass sie neidisch lügenhafft, diebisch und frevel-haft seyn, die da ihren Stieff-Kindern, keinen guten Bissen gönnen, sondern sie verfolgen, und suchen ihnen ihr gehöriges Erbgut zu entziehen. Und hier hat nun das Facit doppelt eingetroffen, und das missgünstige Glück seinen weiten Platz eingenommen, so, dass durch den Fluch Gottes, diese so edle Massa in ein wüstes und verächtliches Kleid, id est die feces terrae, der Sulphurischen und Arsenicalischen Geister, verkleidet wurde. Denn erstens wurden sie aus der obern Region, da sie gebohren worden, verfolget, und in die untersten Regionen herabgesandt, daher sagt Hermes: Der Wind hat ihn in seinen Bauch getragen, oder wie oben gesagt, auf dem goldenen Widder, als dem Golden Vlies, der guten Witterung ist er herab gekommen, darvon sodenn alles sein Leben und Wachsthum erhalten hat. Und Zweytens, wurden diese edle Principien von dem Fluche der Erden überzogen und vergestaltet, dass man sie, ohne einem sohn der Weissheit, nicht kennet, viewohl sie doch allgemein, und aller Orten zu finden ist."

Proposed translation:

The sun, Athamas, the fiery solar sulphur, is the father of this noble *child. For from the sun, from Athamas, flows forth the fiery martian semen, the noble igneous life, the solar tincture, the tincturing spirit, the astral spirit of the higher elements and emanations (*Ausflüsse*). They come down into the child's womb, into its mother, the place of the underworld receptacles, through the moon, Nephelea, that is, the aqueous and lunar outflows (*Augüsse*), and passions. From the moon, indeed, flows out the watery but very fiery and venusian (*venerisch*) semen, the wise lunar mercury, the wise astral spirit, the wise and dry water, which does not wet the hands, the great solvent, the philosophers' Alkahest, in which the philosophers' gold is radically dissolved and made liquid—which nothing else in the world is able to do. It is as if Hermes wanted to tell us that we must know that the sun is a great and mighty planet in the orb of the sky (according to astronomical calculations, 140 times larger than our globe), of a wholly fiery quality, like a great sea of molten metal sending forth its liquid rays [. . .]. Should its rays come straight down upon earth, everything there would be turned into dust and ashes; however, the good Lord has not created anything with a view to its being destroyed; on the contrary, all that he has done is wise and good: just as he created this big planet to warm up the cold and humid earth, its cold and mercurial parts, so did he oppose to the sun the moon, a cold and humid planet which, like a third person hovers between sun and earth, and is 42 times smaller than earth. The sun's fiery rays concentrate in the moon, which takes away their heat; once they are cooler, it sends back to earth these seeds, which have been thus subject to its impregnation. In the same way, Athamas and Nephele, through their nuptial and royal bond, begot two royal children, Phryxos and Helle, that is, a solar sulphur and a lunar mercury. They were born in the kingdom of Thebes, that is, the higher elements and regions, from whence they had to come down: they were driven out of their father's kingdom and monarchy. Indeed, Nephelea, the moon, their mother, of poor or weak constitution, and much too cold, was not able to preserve the semen and products of the sun; so she herself had to withdraw as if she were dead. Some other planets, for their part, and especially Jupiter, had sent a contrary current, that of their feelings and emotions, which were like those of cruel stepmothers and of the mob of priests; under the action of this current of arsenical mercury and sulphur, the children left their dwelling in the higher regions. As if bathed in a shower of holy gold, they had to come down with the Golden Fleece, the great golden Ram, through the air region, down to the etheric earthly cold, upon the earth, and they enjoyed a wonderful welcome*

*in the latter's three principles and elements, that is, in the kingdom
of Colchis.*

*Ino, Athamas' second wife, signified the negative astral aspects
and impressions, originating from Jupiter. Jupiter is a patron of the
mob of priests. That is why it is said that Ino, as a priest's daughter,
might have been fairly good and beneficial to both children; however, she was not there at the beginning of things; she was created,
slipped in, inserted, as a secondary element by the frightening curse
of God only after the fall of Lucifer and Adam. In other words these
arsenical spirits, these "negative impressions" (*widrige Impressiones*), should be understood as a second marriage, considered as
representing a cruel stepmother. It is indeed well-known that all that
comes from the priesthood, from this mob, is most nasty, perverse,
despicable, cunning, flattering, false, pompous, arrogant. Our sav-
iour Jesus Christ himself complains about it when he says again
and again: "Woe to you Pharisees and Doctors of the Law, hypocrites,
serpents, nest of vipers, you will not escape damnation!" (*Matthew
23*). Stepmothers also have a very bad reputation, which follows
them all over the world. They are said to be envious, untruthful, dishonest, and villainous; they don't leave anything good to their poor
children, but persecute them and seek to deprive them of their lawful
heritage. Here, misfortune has doubly struck Phryxos and Helle; it
fell upon a vast area in such a way that, through a divine curse, that
most noble mass (that was the universe) was changed into a despicable wilderness, the faces of the earth, under the influence of these
sulphuric and arsenical spirits. For first, the two persecuted children were driven from the higher regions where they were born and
sent down to the lower regions. That is why Hermes says: "The wind
has borne him in its womb"; or as said above, has borne him on the
golden Ram or Golden Fleece; he has come down from the good at-
mospheric regions, whence he received life and growth. The noble
principles themselves were covered up and distorted by the curse
that had befallen earth, to the point that unless one is a son of
wisdom they cannot be known, although they are everywhere, in all
places.*

12) Louis-Claude de SAINT**-M**ARTIN**.** ***Tableau Naturel des rapports qui
unissnet Dieu, l'homme et l'univers.*** **Paris, 1782, t. I, abstracts from
pages 210 to 220. Cf.** ***supra,*** **page 51:**
"Le but de l'Art hermétique, le plus généralement connu, ne s'élève
jamais au dessus de la matière (. . .) En vain quelques partisans de cette
Science séduisante, prétendent-ils obtenir par elle, une Science plus

noble encore, qui les élèveroit autant au dessus des adeptes matériels,
que ceux-ci le seroient au dessus du vulgaire. Ces hommes, très-
louables dans leurs désirs, cessent de l'être, dès que l'on considèrepar
quelle voie ils cherchent à les remplir. Car une substance quelconque
ne peut produire que des fruits de sa nature: et très certainement les
fruits après lesquels ils semblent soupirer, sont d'une nature bien
différente des substances qu'ils soumettent à leurs manipulations. Si
l'Art hermétique matériel n'atteint pas au-delà des objets matériels, cet
Art n'est pas dans une classe plus élevée que l'Agriculture; il est donc
evident que les emblèmes et les symboles de la Mythologie lui sont
égaement étrangers, puisqu'ils présentent le langage de l'intelligence, et
qu'ils donnent une vie et une action à des facultés qui sont inconnues à
la matière. Ceux qui ont cru voir tant de rapports entre des choses aussi
différentes, ne les ont confondues qu'en se laissant séduire par
l'uniformité des lois qui leur sont communes (. . .) Ce sont ces con-
formités qui ont abusé les Observateurs. Ils ont attribué à des
opérations absolument matérielles, une foule de principes qui ne
pouvoient convenir qu'à des objects supérieurs par leur action et par
toutes les propriétés qui leur sont inhérentes. Par là il est certain qu'ils
ont ravalé les anciens symboles, au lieu de nous les expliquer (. . .) Les
philosophes hermétiques m'ont pas vu que la simple physique matéri-
elle, à laquelle ils ont appliqué tous leurs efforts, ne méritoit point ces
mystères, ni ce langage énigmatique et enveloppé que présentent les
anciens emblémes; ils n'ont pas vu que, s'il existoit une Science digne de
l'étude et des hommages de l'homme, c'étoit celle qui mettoit sa
grandeur en évidence, en l'éclairant sur son origine, et sur l'étendue de
ses facultés naturelles et intellectuelles (. . .) Réunissant à toutes ces
observations la grande loi de l'infériorité que doivent avoir les emblèmes
envers leur type, on reconnoitra que la Philosophie hermétique n'a pu
être le premier but, ni le type réel des allégories de la Fable. Il seroit
contre la vraisemblance, que la nature de l'homme éclairé l'eût porté à
imaginer l'intervention des Divinités, pour voiler une Science qui se
contredit et qui les injurie (. . .) L'homme, son origine, sa fin, la loi qui
doit le conduire à son terme, les causes qui l'en tiennent éloigné, enfin,
la *Science de l'homme,* inséparablement liée à celle du Premier de tous
les Principes, voilà les objets que les Auteurs des Traditions primitives
ont voulu peindre (. . .) En effet, il n'est point d'homme instruit de sa
vraie nature, qui, s'il cherche à pénétrer le sens des Traditions
mythologiques, n'y aperçoive avec une espèce d'admiration, les symboles des faits les plus importants pour l'espèce humaine et les plus
analogues à lui-même."

Proposed translation:

The purpose of the hermetic art most generally acknowledged never rises above matter (. . .) In vain do some followers of this fascinating science claim to obtain from it a still nobler science that would raise them as much above the material adepts as the latter would be raised above the vulgar. These people, to be commended for their desires, can no longer be so as soon as one looks at the path they tread in their attempt to fulfill them. For a substance cannot but produce fruit of its own nature; and certainly the fruit they seem to long for are very different in nature from the substances they choose to manipulate.

If the material hermetic art does not reach beyond material objects, this art does not belong to a higher class than agriculture; therefore it is obvious that the emblems and symbols of mythology are also unknown to it, since they offer the language of intelligence and give a life and an action to faculties unknown to matter.

Those who thought to have discovered so many connections between things so widely different from one another have only, in so doing, let themselves be allured by the uniformity of the laws common to all things (. . .) These conformities have indeed confused the observers. They have ascribed to entirely material operations many principles which could only apply to objects superior by their action and by all the properties inherent to them. Thereby they have certainly disparaged the ancient symbols instead of explaining them to us (. . .) Hermetic philosophers failed to see that the simple material physics, which was their only concern, was not worthy of such secrecy, of this cryptic language, shrouded in mystery, offered by the ancient emblems; they failed to see that, if there was a science deserving to be studied and honored by man, it was that science which brought his greatness in evidence, in shedding some light about his origin and the scope of his natural and intellectual faculties (. . .) Bringing together all these observations with the great law of inferiority which emblems must have for their type, it will become clear that hermetic philosophy could not be the primary goal or the true type of the allegories of the fable. It would be most unreasonable to think that the nature of the enlightened man was such as to make him conceive of the interference of the gods in order to veil a science which is inconsistent with the divine and which abuses it. (. . .) Man, his origin, his purpose, the law that is to lead him to his goal, the reasons for his being kept away from this goal, and finally the science of man, inseparably linked to the science of the first of all principles—such are the objects that the authors of the primitive traditions wanted to depict. (. . .) Indeed, no one knowing his true nature and seeking to gain insight into mythological traditions would fail to discern there, with admiration, symbols of the facts which are the most important to humankind and the most analagous to himself.

APPENDIX 2: A NOTE ON THE GOLDEN FLEECE IN FREEMASONRY

We have seen that some masonic rites borrowed certain designs from the myth of the Golden Fleece. This concerns mainly the Higher Grades, that is, those grades which, in some Rites (known as "scottish") are superimposed upon the first three (Entered Apprentice, Fellow Craftsman and Master Mason, making up the Masonry known as "blue" or "symbolic" or "Craft Masonry"). The higher grades, which have never been of great interest to the English, proliferated on the continent from about 1740 onwards. It may be that some of them, as early as the 1740's, introduced a few elements of the myth of the Golden Fleece into their rituals. Chronologically, the first appearance of the Golden Fleece I have been able to trace so far (although there should have been some others prior to that) dates back to 1761, in a context which is not masonic in the strict sense of the word, but rather para-masonic. It is the German Order of the Golden Rosy Cross—or rather a direct ancestor of the Order of that name, founded shortly afterwards. It relates its masonic legend to the legend of the Golden Fleece, while claiming also to be from the lineage of the Order of the Temple.[1]

George Walnon, a Scotsman, is said to have founded on April 4, 1751 a lodge in Marseille, called Saint-Jean d'Ecosse. Some time after (perhaps ten years later, therefore contemporary to the German rosicrucian reference quoted *supra*), this Lodge had 18 Higher Degrees, the tenth being "Knight of the Argonauts," and the eleventh "Knight of the Golden Fleece.,, Of these eighteen grades we know only the names (1bis).

A few years later there appears in France a rite called "Hermetic Rite," about which some information is available. Since reputations shape reactions, it is the name of Dom Pernety that was associated with the creation, in Avignon, of this new masonic system, the number of its lodges being unknown to us. Actually Pernety is by no means its founder. This mistake may be due to the fact that Pernety had gathered about him a number of followers in an esoteric society—called the "Illuminati of Avignon"—some of whom, such as Dr. Bouge, were also members of the Hermetic Rite.[2] Pernety did not set foot in this town until 1784. But as early as 1774, the grades of this rite are well attested, and in a way that leads us to assume that their creation might date back to the late 1760's. It was probably organized locally, in Avignon, and is of interest here, for among its seventeen grades we find those of Knight of the Argonauts and Knight of the Golden Fleece. In a letter dated 1774 and addressed to the Grand Orient, a brother from Avignon called Saint-Léger states that he is invested with these seventeen grades. The founder is probably Charles-Michel-Jean-Louis Toussaint, marquis d'Aigrefeuille, a gentleman from Montpellier who, in 1778, introduced this Rite in his own town, in a Chapter of the Golden Fleece.[3] This Chapter seems to represent a modification when compared to the early Hermetic Rite, for henceforth five Higher Grades are distinguished (and no longer fourteen or seventeen), namely: the true Mason in the Straight Way, the Knight of the Golden Key, the Knight of the Iris, the Knight of the Argonauts, and the Knight of the Golden Fleece. Brother Thory, to whom we owe this information, writes in 1812:

> All these grades are a superfluity of the grade of the Academy of the True Masons and offer, similarly, an emblematic explanation of the operations indicated by the hermetic philosophers and leading to the discovery of the philosophers' stone and the universal medicine. The chapter of the Knights of the Golden Fleece of Montpellier gives the constitution of the lodges to which these types of knowledge are agreeable. It seems to have found a few establishments of this kind in France.
>
> We know that, on March 5th, 1785, this chapter established an Academy of the True Masons in Saint-Pierre, Isle of Martinique. That Academy was established on the following June 18th by Mr. Goyer de Jumilly. Here is a fragment of the speech he delivered: "To take hold of Hermes' chisel to engrave on your columns the elements of natural philosophy; to call to my assistance Flamel, the Philalethe, the Cosmopolitan, and our other masters, in order to reveal to you the mysterious principles of occult sciences; such seem to be, illustrious knights, wise academicians, the duties laid upon me by the ceremony of your installation . . . The fountain of the Count of Trevisan, the poetic water, the peacock's tail, are familiar phenomena to us. . . . We shall be able to appraise the doctrine of the Montpellier Lodge from this passage we discovered in the archives of the G.O. of France, a record of the Lodge of Saint-Pierre, Isle of Martinique."[4]

At this time, that is, on the eve of the revolution, the rite had already spread to other chapters in Switzerland, Prussia, and Russia.[5] But this is not the end of its story; from several documents we can follow its traces during the Empire. Mostly, the story is found in the correspondence exchanged between a Swedish gentleman named Jean-Etienne-Juste d'Hermensen, and a famous Mason, the Marquis of Chefdebien. At this time, in 1806, the Hermetic Rite had become the Rite of Saint Alexander of Scotland. In a letter dated May 12th, d'Hermensen, who claims he belongs to it, points out to Chefdebien the grades he achieved there: General of the Argonauts and Knight of the Argonauts.[6] Forced to justify himself before Chefdebien (regarding another issue, whose nature is not relevant here), d'Hermensen states that his good faith is based on his belonging to Masonry: "I shall support what I shall suggest by the authenticity of the august mysticism I make use of in all my mas. correspondences . . . as Kn. of the Golden Fleece and representative of the grades of Wisdom with the Orients of Northern Europe."[7] In the same letter he states that there "can only be twelve Knights of the Golden Fleece, and that each has for an indelible and distinctive sign one of the twelve zodiacal signs." And he adds: "The sign which has been given to me always appears along with my signature." It is in Germany, not in France, that d'Hermensen was received into the Chapters of the Order of the "Hermetic Masonry." Furthermore, he writes on July 12th, these chapters "already had gathered rich and precious harvests."[8]

However, d'Hermensen was disappointed by the French masonic life, on grounds which he discusses throughout this fine passage, in which he also tells about his admission to the French Chapter of Saint Alexander of Scotland:

> I had given up, since my return to Paris, the exercise of the Mas[onry] in France, because I was fully conscious (and I am more and more so every day) of its uselessness. The Mas. needs not only some mystery, but above all meditative and fervent men attaching to the revelations they obtain all the importance they deserve and who, full of respect for their Order, of friendliness for their Brothers, and of interest for humanity, devote themselves with some kind of zest to this same Order.
>
> I would even venture to say, my most worthy Brother, that the French nation, so pleasant otherwise, so full of wit and graces as to social relations, usually brings so much flightiness in all her doings, that the most serious matters become, so to say, quite funny every time she wants to deal with such practices. So the Mas. is what it really *is* only in Germany and in a few northern coun-

tries. There these thinking and thoughtful souls, duly appreciating the good, engage themselves with respect, assiduity and zeal in the cultivation of this vast field, open to all through the grace from above: a field so fertile when cultivated by hard-working hands, so full of brambles and thorns when the seed is allowed to be choked by useless weeds.

To close this already lengthy digression and return to my own self, I was then, as I have just said, keeping away from any mas. practice. Everything is a fashion in Paris, from pompoms to mas., and from *opéra comique* to feeling. So the lodges have been opened; the great names brought there the plates and ribbons they have received from every country, and amidst the profusion of decorations (for the Masons of Paris have plenty of them), we are at a loss to ascertain the use of these baubles, to which the dear servants of the Grand-Orient attach such a great value. Before long we wouldn't hear about anything but Mas., and everyone, from the great names of the Empire to the office clerks, has rushed en masse into the lodges.

The Lodge of Saint Alexander of Scotland, thinking it could discern in me some degree of learning, admitted me within itself, and I must say to its credit that all the grades were bestowed on me at once and, taken to the top, without any financial contribution, I accepted. The composition of this Parent Lodge, a rehash from Avignon, as you said so pleasantly in one of your dispatches, prompts me to join it. Almost all the Mas. meetings, in Paris, are such that one should consider oneself fortunate to find again one's handkerchief and snuffbox in their allocated pocket.

Saint Alexander is composed of honest and decent people who, if lacking means, at least are not lacking in consideration and politeness. I would go so far as to say: this Lodge should be set apart from most others (for in the kingdom of the blind the one-eyed man is king), because at least the rite it teaches, although it tends to be very successful, still remains a rite. The summit of this majestic building (for, in our modesty, we give him unhesitatingly this pompous name) is the chap[ter] of the Golden Fleece, which this Lodge, so learned in its own words, owes to the bounty of Br[other] d'Aigrefeuille, who made it.

In the grades of this chap., after a quite well-reasoned study of metals, we urge the neophyte to put into practice the very clear processes handed down to us by the hermetic philosophers; and all we can do is teach them that we believe in the feasibility of the great work; that in truth we do not know anything about matter and fire, but that apart from this we are very learned: that illuminations are only with us; that they cannot be found elsewhere and that they should be eternally grateful for the happy day when we passed on to them such a unique secret. Here we are, then, center of centers, receiving from all quarters the names of Almighty, Most Wise, Most Illustrious, and hurling them ourselves at each other most foolishly.

You will appreciate—I have no doubt about it—the behavior of Dear Brother d'Aigrefeuille: it is all the more noble and disinterested as, even though he was curious like every seeker and jealous as President of the Chap.·. of the Golden Fleece to see the lodge provided with illuminations, he went out of his way to stop Br.·. Thory in his indiscreet race. Br.·. d'Aigrefeuille is the only one of us who has some hermetic knowledge, and to him, as I have mentioned above, we owe this Ch.·. of the 12, of which he had been a member, in Montpellier, for thirty-three years, and such an active one.[9]

In 1809 the Hermetic Rite was placed under the authority of a Grand Master, and under its shade many other rites had to submit Cambacérès, "Protector" of the French Lodges.[10] Henceforth, if this system born in Avignon does not seem to have flourished much, the Golden Fleece, for its part, reappears in new rites. Not, it seems, in the Misraim Rite, spread in France from 1814 onward through the efforts of the three Bédarride brothers—and Brothers!—(Michel, Joseph, and Marc), also, and coincidentally, from Avignon; but in its rival, the Memphis Rite, which was just as influenced by egyptomania as the former. It was born in 1815 in Montauban, and is mostly the work of Marconis de Nègre, and later of his son Jacques-Etienne Marconis. The last Memphis grades are permeated by Egyptianism; they repeat, almost to the letter, the nomenclature of Misraim in its final classes, from the seventy-eighth to the eighty-ninth degree (there are, depending on the versions, ninety or ninety-five of them!), apart from two degrees, including the eightieth, that of Knight of the Golden Fleece. Rituals have varied, but according to Gérard Galtier, who went through some portions of these documents, the grade of Knight of the Golden Fleece, sometimes also called Sublime Prince of the Golden Fleece, was generally at the eightieth degree of the hierarchy. It is found at the fifty-second degree in *L'Hiérophante,* a precious wealth of information on this masonic system published in 1839 by Marconis.[11] It is also found, this time at the tenth degree, in *Le Rameau d'Or d'Eleusis* (1861) by the same author, a book which also gives many details about these grades.[12]

In addition, in Memphis there is a 'symbolic' decoration known as the Golden Fleece, of which we could not trace any specimen. This is however an actual grade; that is, not only formal or abstractly mentioned in a series of other grades conferred at the same time, for a piece of information published in *L'Hiérophante* announced its publication. But it seems the promise was not kept.[13] Nevertheless, by way of illustration, here is Marconis' description of this tenth grade (or degree), that of Knight of the Golden Fleece, as published in 1861 in *Le Rameau d'Or d'Eleusis:*

> *Sign.* Putting the right hand on the pommel of one's sword, and whisking it away horizontally.
>
> *Touch.* Clasping each other's right hand and pressing it three times.
>
> *Beat.* Seven equal beats.
>
> *Walk.* Ordinary walk.
>
> *Password. Beamacheh Bamcarah* (Thank God!)
>
> *Sacred word. Darakiel* (direction of God).
>
> *Insignia and ornaments.* Silk scarf, orange-colored, with golden fringes; one ponceau cord, worn round the neck, with an embroidered golden fleece within a silver glory; the tunic is sky-blue.[14]

In 1876, the merging of both the rites into a third one, known as Memphis-Misraim, has of course deeply altered the order, and mostly the nature, of some of their grades. However, that of Knight of the Golden Fleece is still there, at the tenth degree. But in the latest reform of Memphis-Misraim, which dates from 1980, the first thirty-three degrees have been aligned with the Ancient and Accepted Scottish Rite, so that this grade has now disappeared. Were the adepts of the revised Memphis-Misraim Rite aware, twelve years ago, that they were thus erasing one of the degrees which made for the attractiveness, originality, and to some extent, traditional value of this conferment of grades?[15]

Finally, it is probably in the very early years of the nineteenth century that the Rite of the Parent Lodge of Marseille began to practice a number of higher grades of a marked hermetical and alchemical nature, including those of Knight of the Argonauts and Knight of the Golden Fleece (respectively the eleventh and twelfth of the nineteen grades of this system).[16]

———————————— *Notes to Appendix 2* ————————————

1. Cf. Wolfstieg's *Masonic Bibliography,* nr.42598: *"Die älteste Orden-slegende der Rosenkreuzer,* 1761: Nach einem MS. des Br. J. Ritz-Tramopidomus im Archiv zu Dégh (Bd.61, Nr1). Die Ordenssage der neuen G. oder R.K. lehnt sich an die Sage vom goldenen Vliess an und leitet die Abstammung des Orders direkt von den Tempelherren ab. In: O. 1887, S.124-125." The Dégh archives, formerly owned by the Festetich family, are now at the Budapest Landesarchiv. Abafi, the historian of Austrian Masonry, seems to refer to this in his article "Die Entstehung der Gold- und Rosenkreuzer" (p. 82 f. in *Latomia,* XXII, 1900): he mentions a text of the year 1761, belonging to a Lodge in Prague and entitled *Aureum vellus seu Iunioratus Fratrum Rosae Crucis.* This text is in part copied from Fictuld's book of 1749 (see also Arnold Max "Die Gold- und Rosenkreuzer," p. 17 in *Das Freimaurer Museum,* Band V, 1930). In Germany, these Rosicrucians (i.e., the members of the Order of the Gold and Rosy Cross) are interested in the symbolism of the Golden Fleece well into the eighties. A classic in Rosicrucian literature, *Compass der Weisen* (Berlin and Leipzig, 1779; 2nd edition, 1782), has a passage in which we learn that the inhabitants of Colchis had the same religion as their Egyptian ancestors, the same language and the same sciences. Their Egyptian legacy in terms of science is proved by their Golden Fleece, which is a book : "ein Buch, in welchem die Kunst, das grosse Universal der Welt, mit allen seinen Heilungsh und Verwandlungskräften, nach der von ihren Stammvätern erlernten Art, NB umständlich beschrieben stund." The author goes on saying that the members of the higher grades of the Order of the Gold and Rosy Cross are true "Toisonists," and he quotes Mennens and Fictuld (p. 71 f.).

1. bis. Interestingly, the 18th is called "Knight of the Sun," and the 13th "Knight Adept of the Eagle and of the Sun" (on the knighthood of the Sun, cf. *infra* note 89). On this rite with 18 Higher Degrees, cf. Georg Kloss, *Geschichte der Freimaurerei in Frankreich, aus echten Urkunden dargestellt 1725-1830.* Darmstadt: Jonghaus, 1852/53 (reprint: Graz: Akad. Druck- und Verlagsanstalt, 1971), t.I, p. 77. Karl R. H. Frick has quoted these grades in his book *Licht und Finsternis,* t.II, Graz: Akad. Druck- und Verlagsanstalt, 1978, p. 60. I find this list of 18 grades very much similar to a list presented in a masonic manuscript of the 18th century entitled *Collection d'un Amateur. Livres et précieux manuscrits maçonniques,* sold at an auction sale in Paris in 1987 and published thereafter by Arma Artis Editions (Paris, s.d.) under the title *Tous les rituels alchimiques du Baron de Tschoudy.* On this manuscript and the publication at Arma Artis', cf. Pierre Mollier's valuable work, quoted *infra,* note 89 (p. 105 f. of his dissertation).

2. Cf. A) Micheline Meillassoux-Le-Cerf's doctoral dissertation, quoted *infra,* note 129. B) Robert Amadou's article in *Dictionnaire Universel de la Franc-Maçonnerie* (published by Daniel Ligou). Paris, P.U.F., 1787, pp. 909-914. C) Thory. *Annales originis magni Gallorum O . . ., ou Histoire de*

la Fondation du Grand Orient de France. Paris, 1812, p. 199 f. D) Gustave Bord. *La Franc-Maçonnerie en France, des origines à 1815,* T.I, Paris, 1919, p. 258 f. Bord's and Thory's confusions about Pernety's and Masonry are refuted by Amadou and Meillassoux-Le-Cerf. But in the printed edition of her work (Paris, Ed. Arché, 1992), Meillassoux-Lecerf has inserted a note by André Boyer, who had just discovered some new material documenting Pernety's actual membership in Freemasonry.

3. Amadou, article quoted note *supra*, p. 913.

4. Thory, *op. cit.* pp. 199 f. *"Tous ces grades sont une superfétation de celui de l'Académie des Vrais Maçons, et offrent, comme lui, une explicitation emblématique des opérations indiquées par les philosophes hermétiques pour parvenir à la découverte de la pierre philosophale et de la médecine universelle. Le chapitre des chevaliers de la Toison d'Or de Montpellier donne les constitutions des Loges auxquelles ces sortes de connaissances sont agréables. Il paraît avoir formé quelques établissements de ce genre en France.*

Nous savons que, le 5 mars 1785, il a constitué une Académie des Vrais Maçons, à Saint-Pierre, île de la Martinique. Elle a été installée le 18 juin suivant par M. Goyer de Jumilly. Voici un fragment du discours qu'il adressa à l'assemblée après la cérémonie de l'inauguration: "Saisir le burin d'Hermès pour graver sur vos colonnes les éléments de la philosophie naturelle; appeler à mon aide Flamel, le Philalèthe, le Cosmopolite et nos autres maîths, pour vos dévoiler les principes mystérieux des sciences occultes, tels semblent être, illustres chevaliers, sages académiciens, les devoirs que m'impose la cérémonie de votre installation... La fontaine du comte de Trévisan, l'eau poétique, la queue du paon, sont des phénomènes qui nous sont familiers[...] On pourra juger de la doctrine de la Loge de Montpellier par ce passage que nous avons extrait dans les archives du G.O. de France, dossier de la Loge de Saint-Pierre, île de la Martinique."[4]

5. *Ibid.* p. 200: "Prior to the Revolution, the Chapter of the Golden Fleece was in correspondence with the members of its system in Prussia, in Sweden, and in Russia. It still calls its Academy (its grade being the only one that can be regarded as ancient and genuine) by the name of *Russo-Swedish* Academy. The oldest academy of the *True Masons* known in the Order, is the academy still in existence in Avignon, within the Lodge of the Persecuted Virtue. *Dom Pernetti* was one of its members; among them were a great number of French and foreign scholars. The academy once connected to the Lodge of the *Contrat Social* belonged to its constitution, as witnessed by the old manuscript from the archives of this P[arent] L[odge]."

6. Letter of May 12th, 1806: "one of the unique 12 of this S∴ C∴ with the typical ✚." In: Benjamin Fabre. *Un Initié des Sociétés Secrètes supérieures, Franciscus, Eques A Capite Galeato (1753–1814).* Paris; La Renaissance Française, 1913, p. 373.

7. *Ibid.*, June 1806, p. 378.

8. *Ibid.*, July 1806, p. 388.

9. *Ibid.*, letter dated "28…1806", pp. 400–403. We also learn, p. 402, that Thory recruits for Saint Alexander of Scotland, and that the marquis d'Aigrefeuille is still President of the Chapter of the Golden Fleece. Text: *"J'avais abandonné, depuis mon retour à Paris l'exercice de la Maç. en France, parce que j'étais pénétré (et je le suis tous les jours davantage) de sa nullité. La Maç. veut non seulement du mystère, mais surtout des hommes recueillis et fervents, qui attachent aux révélations qu'ils obtiennent toute l'importance qu'elles méritent, et qui, pénétrés de respect pour leur Ordre, d'amitié pour leurs Frères, et d'intérêt pour l'humanité, se vouent avec une sorte d'enthousiasme à ce même Ordre.*

Oserai-je le dire, Mon Très Digne Frère, la nation française, si aimable d'ailleurs, si pleine d'esprit et de grâces, quant aux rapports sociaux, apporte en général une si grande légèreté dans tout ce qu'elle fait, que les choses les plus sérieuses deviennent, pour ainsi dire risibles, dès qu'elle veut se mêler de semblables pratiques. Aussi la Maç. n'est-elle réellement ce qu'elle est, qu'en Allemagne, et dans quelques contrées du Nord. Là, ces esprits, penseurs et réfléchis, justes appréciateurs du bon, se livrent avec respect, assiduité et zèle, à la culture de ce vaste champ, ouvert à tous par la grâce d'en haut: champ si fécond, lorsqu'il est travaillé par des mains laborieuses, si plein de ronces, et d'épines, lorsqu'on laisse étouffer la semence par les végétations inutiles.

Pour terminer cette digression, déjà trop prolongée, et en revenir à moi, j'étais donc, comme je viens de le dire, éloigné de toute pratique maç. Tout est de mode, à Paris, depuis les pompons, jusqu'à la ma., et depuis l'opéra-comique, jusqu'au sentiment. Les Loges se sont donc ouvertes; les grands personnages y ont apporté les plaques et les cordons qu'ils ont reçus de tous les pays, et, dans cette confusion de décorations (car les Maçons de Paris n'en manquent pas) on a peine à distinguer ce qui est civil de ces brimborions auxquels Messieurs les serviteurs du Grand-Orient attachent un si grand prix. Bientôt on n'a plus entendu parler que de Maç., et depuis les grands de l'Empire jusqu'aux commis de Bureau tout s'est précipité en masse dans les Loges.

Celle de Saint-Alexandre d'Ecosse, croyant apercevoir en moi quelque instruction, me fit entrer dans son sein, et je dois le dire à sa louange, tous les grades me furent accordés à l'instant, et porté au faîte, sans aucune contribution pécuniaire, j'acceptai. La composition de cette Mère Loge, réchauffée d'Avignon, comme vous l'avez plaisamment dit, dans une de vos dépêches, m'engage à me réunir à elle. Presque toutes les réunions Mac., à Paris, sont telles que l'on doit se trouver heureux, en sortant, de retrouver son mouchoir et sa tabatière dans la poche où on les tient.

Saint-Alexandre est composé de gens honnêtes et decents qui, s'ils sont sans moyens, ne sont pas au moins sans égard et sans politesse. Je dirai plus: cette Loge doit être distinguée de la plupart des autres (car, au royaume des aveugles, les borgnes sont des rois), parce qu'au moins le Rit, qu'elle professe, tend à un qui, pour être presque idéal, quant à la réussite, n'en est pas moins un. Le comble de ce majestueux édifice (car, dans notre modestie, nous n'hésitons pas à lui donner ce nom pompeux) est le Chap. de la Toison d'Or, que cette Loge si instruite, à ce qu'elle dit, doit aux bontés du F∴ d'Aigrefeuille, qui l'a constituée.

Dans les grades de ce Chap., après une analyse assez bien raisonée des métaux, nous engageons les néophytes à mettre en œuvre les procédés si clairs, que nous ont transmis les philosophes hermét.∴; et tout notre savoir se réduit à les instruire que nous croyons à la possibilité du grand œuvre; qu'à la vérité nous ignorons la matière et le feu, mais, qu'à cela près, nous sommes très savants: que les lumières ne sont que chez nous; qu'on les chercherait en vain ailleurs, et qu'ils doivent bénir, à jamais, le jour heureux où nous leur avons transmis un aussi rare secret. Nous voilà donc ainsi foyer des foyers, recevant de partout les noms de Très-puissants, Très Sages, Très Illustres, et nous les jetant nous-mêmes, fort sottement à la tête les uns des autres.

Vous apprécierez—je n'en doute point—la conduite du Ch∴F∴ d'Aigre-feuille: elle est d'autant plus noble et plus désintéressée que, curieux comme tous les chercheurs, et jaloux comme Président du Chap∴, de la Toison d'Or, de voir la Loge pourvue de lumières, il a mis tout en œuvre pour arrêter le F∴ Thory dans sa course indiscrète. Le F∴ d'Aigrefeuille est le seul d'entre nous qui possède des connaissances hermétiques, et c'est à lui, comme je l'ai dit plus haut, que nous devons ce Chap∴des 12, dont il était membre à Montpellier, depuis trente-trois ans, et membre travaillant."[9]

10. Thory, *op. cit.,* p. 201

11. Cf. Gastone Ventura. *I Riti Massonici di Misraïm e Memphis,* 1975, French translation by Gérard Galtier: *Les Rites de Memphis et de Misraïm.* Paris: Maisonneuve-Larose, 1986, p. 68. And Gérard Galtier: *La Franc-Maçonnerie Egyptienne en France de 1783 à 1983.* Monaco: Le Rocher, 1989.

12. J.E. Marconis. *Le Rameau d'Or d'Eleusis.* Paris: with the author, 1861.

13. Cf. *L'Hiérophante,* 1839. On the promise not kept, a letter from Gérard Galtier to myself, 5th October 1988.

14. *Le Rameau d'Or d'Eleusis* (cf. *supra,* note 12), p. 413:
"Signe. *Porter la main droite sur la paume de son épée, et la retirer horizontalement avec vivacité.*
Attouchement. *Se donner mutellement la main droite et la presser par trois fois.*
Batterie. *Sept coups égaux.*
Marche. *Marche ordinaire.*
Parole de passe. Beamacheh Bamcarah *(Dieu soit loué!).*
Parole sacrée. *Darakiel (direction de Dieu).*

Insignes et décors. *Echarpe en soie, couleur d'orange, avec frange en or; un cordon ponceau, porté en sautoir, sur lequel est brodée une toison d'or dans une gloire en argent; la tunique est bleu-céleste."[14]*

15. Information provided by Gérard Galtier in the letter referred to *supra*, note 13. Let us note, in response, that this title of the Golden Fleece is the distinctive title of the Grande Loge Féminine de France à l'Orient de Dijon, and of a Lodge of the Loge Nationale Française à l'Ouest de Lille; cf. Daniel Ligou's *Dictionnaire* (referred to *supra*, note 2), p. 995.

16. *Dictionnaire Universel de la Franc-Maçonnerie* (cf. *supra*, note 2), p. 1015.

Notes

1. On myth and history, cf. among the recent publications: *Le Mythe et le Mythique*. Paris, Albin Michel, collection "Bibliothèque de l'Hermétisme" (Proceedings of the Colloquium of Cerisy-la-Salle, July 1985). This collective work includes a summary of my article "D'Hermès-Mercure à Hermès Trismégiste: au confluent du Mythe et du Mythique," published in full in the "Cahier" of the same collection entitled *Présence d'Hermès Trismégiste*, in 1989 (cf. pp. 24–28). An English version of this article is forthcoming (in *The Eternal Hermes*, a selection of articles by A. Faivre on Hermes. Grand Rapids (M), Phanes Press, 1993).

2. It should also be noted that the rape of Europe—Agenor's daughter—by Zeus in the form of a winged creature, and Agenor's children, including Cadmus, setting out in search of her, are reminiscent of the myth of the golden ram.

3. For the theme of Agenor in an alchemical context, cf. for instance Michael Maier. *Symbola aureae mensae duodecim nationum*, Frankfurt/ Main, 1617, reed. facsimile: Graz: Akad. Druck- u. Verlagsanstalt, 1972, cf. p. 33 ff.

4. See the collective work *Les Pèlerins de l'Orient et les vagabonds de l'Occident*. Paris: Berg International, collection "Cahiers de Saint Jean de Jérusalem," # IV, 1978.

5. Baron of Reiffenberg. *Histoire de l'Ordre de la Toison d'Or*, Brussels, 1830, p. 21.

6. Martial, 9, 61, 4. Virgil, *Eneid*, VI, 209.

7. Henry Corbin. *En Islam iranien*. Paris: Gallimard, "Bibliothèque des Idées," t.II, 1971, pp. 81 ff.

8. *Ibid.*, t.II, pp. 142 ff.

9. I am grateful to Paul-Georges Sansonetti who pointed out for me this possible connection with the *xvarnah*. Since that time, I have written about this aspect. Cf. "Miles Redivivus," in A. Faivre. *Accès de l'ésotérisme occidental.*

Paris: Gallimard, "Bibliothèque des Sciences Humaines," 1986, pp. 208-234. An English translation of this article is forthcoming (in the American edition of *Accès...* by SUNY Press, 1993).

10. Cf. the French edition: *Le Roman de Troie de Benoît de Sainte-Maure,* translated and presented by Emmanuelle Baumgartner. Paris: Union Générale d'Editions, série 10/18, collection "Bibliothèque Mèdiévale," 1987. Among those who continued in the tradition of Benoît, let us mention Guido delle Colonne (*Historia destructionis Troie,* 1287).

11. *Le roman de Troie,* cited edition (cf. the preceding note), pp. 154, 163.

12. Boccacio. *De genealogia deorum,* Basel edition, 1532, pp. 85, 253, and more importantly 337 f. (a compendium of Jason's venture, without any elaboration on the Ram and his fleece).

13. In my discussion of Fictuld, I mentioned various items of the Order's symbols, especially the coats; cf. "Miles Redivivus," cited *supra,* note 9. The quotation regarding the word *"agnutes"* is in René Alleau. *De la nature des symboles,* Paris: Flammarion, 1958, pp. 105 f. Philip the Good's interest in Jason can be partly explained by the Argonauts' expedition taking place quite close to those places where John the Fearless had fought and lived in captivity. It seems that this interest went beyond the chivalric Order, for shortly before its establishment, Philip had a room arranged in the Hesdin where the story of Jason and Medea was represented. William Caxton, the English translator and publisher of Raoul Lefèvre's book in 1477, writes in his prologue to the book: "But well wote I that the noble Duc Philippe firste founder of this sayd'ordre/dyd' doo maken a chambre in the Castell of Hesdyn/where in was craftyly and curiously depeynted' the conqueste of the golden flese by the said' Jason/in whiche chambre I have ben 'and' seen the sayde historie so depeynted & in remembrance of Medea & har connynck & science, he had do make in the sayde chambreby subtil engyn that whan he wolde it shuld seme that it lightened & then thondre/snowe & rayne. And' all within the sayde chambre as ofte tymes & whan it shuld please him. Which was al made for his singuler pleasir. . . ." (W. Caxton. *Prologue to the History of Jason,* p. 2 of John Munro's edition, London, 1913. Quoted by Victor Tourneur. "Les origines de l'Ordre de la Toison d'or et la symboliques des insignes de celui-ci," pp. 300-315, in: *Bulletin de la classe des Lettres et Sciences Morales et Politiques,* 5éme série, t.XLII, 1956).

14. Elle "est le haut don d'honneur insupérable / qu'on porte en soi, passant mainte traverse / Là sus ès cieux en la gloire durable."

15. Cf. Georges Doutrepont. "Jason et Gédéon, patrons de la Toison d'Or," pp. 191-208 in: *Mélanges Godefroid Kurth.* Liège: Vaillant Larmanne, 1908. And more importantly, Gert Pinkernell. *Raoul Lefèvre: L'histoire de Jason. Ein Roman aus dem 15 Jahrhundert.* Frankfurt/Main: Athenäum, 1971 (for the story of the parchment, cf. p. 183 f.)

16. On Geoffroy de Thoisy (1418-1472), cf. Joseph Calmette. *Les Grands Ducs de Bourgogne.* Paris: Albin Michel, 1976, pp. 22 f. (the first edition is dated 1949). But, most importantly, cf. Baron Paul de Thoisy and E. Nolin. *La Maison de Thoisy au Duché de Bourgogne.* Dijon, 1948, p. 74. Philip the Good's statement in 1461 is taken from: René Alleau, *op. cit.* (*supra,* note 13), p. 103. About the banquet of the Pheasant, cf. Jean de la Croix-Bouton. "Un poème à Philippe le Bon sur la Toison d'Or," in *Annales de Bourgogne,* t.XLII, January –June 1970, p. 6, note 2: "The pledge upon a pheasant was not a mere buffoonery, but a traditional rite. Moreover, pheasant (Greek *Phasanios*) derives from Phasis, a river in Colchis. According to tradition, this bird had been brought to the West by Jason's companions."

17. "Jam regnaverat in Colchis Salauces et Esubopos, qui terram virginem nactus, plurimum argenti aurique erudisse dicitur in Samnorum gente, et alioquin velleribus aureis inclyto regno" (Book XXXIII, ch. 15). F.X.M. Zippe, in *Geschichte der Metalle* (Vienna, 1857), p. 45, observes that in some regions river gold was actually collected by means of skins, their bristly hairs retaining gold particles suspended in water. Quoted by Hermann Kopp. *Geschichte der Chemie.* Brunswick, 1843, t.I, p. 24. Friedrich Joseph Wilhelm Schröder, in *Geschichte der ältesten Chemie und Philosophie oder sogenannten hermetischen Philosophie der Egyptier* (Marburg, 1775, p. 347), also renders *"terra virgo"* by *"jungfräuliche Erde,"* certainly a more esoteric interpretation of what Pliny really meant.

18. On these interpretations, cf. Robert Halleux (to whom I am indebted for the relevant information): a) his doctoral dissertation *La métallurgie des métaux non ferreux dans l'antiquité,* typescript, University of Liège, 1979, pp. 148 f. (about Strabon); b) volume II of the *Greek Alchemists,* text edited and translated by Robert Halleux, to be published by "Les Belles Lettres," Paris (about the Byzantine authors). In this vol. II the references will be found (§ 262 p. 186 ed. Flach, Teubner; commentary to Denys Périégit, 689, p. 340 Müller, Geographia Graeci Maiores, Charax fragment 14 Müller, pp. 324f. Müller). Cf. also Hermann Kopp, *op. cit.,* t. I, pp. 12 ss, quoting about John of Antioch: *Salmasii Plinianae exercitationes in Solini polyhistoria* (Paris, 1629, p. 1097), and from the Suidas the 1853 ed. of the latter's *Lexicon* (ed. G. Bernhardy, Halle et Brunswick, t.I., p. 1212). On these authors and their interpretations of mythology, cf. also Sylvain Matton's valuable study "L'Herméneutique alchimique de la Fable antique," an introduction to Dom Pernety's *Fables Egyptiennes et Grecques dévoilées* (1786 edition). Paris: La Table d'Emeraude, 1982, t.I, pp. 1-2 (no pagination). One should also consult François Secret's article, "Gianfrancesco Pico della Mirandola, Lilio Gregorio Giraldi et l'alchimie," p. 93-112, in: *Bibliothèque d'Humanisme et Renaissance.* Geneva, t.38 (cf. notably the list of cited ancient authors p. 97). As a matter of curiosity, let us mention a recent interpretation suggested by Haroun Tazieff: "Caucasus is a region of volcanoes, now lying dormant; but it was active during antiquity. Jason, in search of the Golden Fleece, sowed dragon's teeth out of which hosts of humans sprang up into existence; could these mean the showers of volcanic

ashes, burning everything but at the same time producing fertile and rapidly exhausted soils?" (Haroun Tazieff. "L'Esprit d'Empédocle," p. 218, note 1, in *Cratères en Feu.*Paris: Club du Bibliophile, 1970 ed.).

19. Cf. in the rest of the present work.

20. The text of the Suidas is taken from his *Lexicon,* ed. A. Adler, Leipzig, 1931, II, 24,21: cf.Δέφας. Already quoted by H.M.E. De Jong. *Michael Maier's Atalanta Fugiens. Source of an alchemical book of emblems.* Leyde: Brill, 1969, p. 309. The text of Eudocia Augusta is quoted by Sylvain Matton (article cited, p. 3). I am grateful for permission to make use of his translation here.

21. Cf. reference in *ibid.* (Sylvain Matton), pp. 3-7.

22. Maso Finiguerra. *A Florentine Picture Chronicle being a Series of ninety-nine Drawings representing Scenes and Personages of Ancient History Sacred and Profane* (Reproduced from the originals in the British Museum by the Imperial Press. Berlin, with a critical and descriptive text by Sidney Colvin). London, Bernard Quaritch, 1898.

23. Cf. Eugène Canseliet. *Deux logis alchimiques. En marge de la science et de l'histoire.* Paris: Pauvert, 1979, pp. 141-316 (cf. mostly pp. 195 f.).

24. Cf. Fulcanelli. *Le mystère des cathédrales et l'interprétation ésotérique des symboles hermétiques du Grand Oeuvre.* Third edition, Paris: Pauvert, 1964, pp. 182-207 (cf. mostly p. 194-196). The first edition is dated 1925.

25. Giovanni Aurelio Augurelli. *Chrysopoeia libri III. Et Geronticon Liber Primus,* Venice, 1515, reed. Basel, 1518. Reprinted in *Theatrum Chemicum* (t.III, 1659, pp. 197 ff.). *Chrysopoeia et Vellus Aureum,* reprinted in Manget (t.II, 1702, pp. 371 ff.). German translation by Valentin Weigel (Hamburg, 1716, reprinted in the 1782 *Hermetisches Museum,* t.II, p. 3). About the ed., cf. Ferguson's t.I, pp. 55 f. French ed.: *Les trois livres de la chrysopée.* Paris, 1626. The story behind the poem is itself something of an odyssey. For the allusion to the Pope's present, cf. Hermann Kopp. *Die Alchemie in älterer und neuerer Zeit. Ein Beitrag zur Kulturgeschichte.* Heidelberg: Karl Winter, 1886, t.I., p. 244. Aloisius Marlianus' address is entitled *Oratio in comitiis ordinis Aurei velleris serenissimi Caroli regis catholici aedita,* 7 pp. + 1 with a blazon. Paris National Library, classification number M 11483.

26. Illustrations presented by Jacques Van Lennep. *Alchimie (Contribution à l'histoire de l'art alchimique).* Brussels and Paris: Crédit Communal de Belgique, and Dervy Livres, 1985 (second edition), pp. 99 and 102.

27. In one volume, in Latin, in 1548. Published in Manget, t.I, pp. 556 ff. Cf. also Sylvain Matton, article cited, pp. 11-13.

28. Bracesco, *op. cit.,* pp. 71f., pp. 43 f.

29. *De Auro libri tres. Opus sane aureum in quo de Auro tum aestimando, tum conficiendo, tum utendo, ingeniose et docte dissertitur.* Venice, 1586 (reed. in 1587 and 1598). To be found in *Theatrum Chemicum* (II, 312 ff.) and in Manget (II, 558 ff.). Consult the bio-bibliography in Ferguson (II, 202 ff.).

30. *De Deis gentium varia et multiplex historia in qua simul de eorum imaginibus et cognominibus agitur,* Basel, 1548.

31. Lilio Giraldi. *Dialogismi XXX.* Venice, 1552. François Secret has published extensive passages from this book, notably the account of this dialogue (cf. article cited *supra,* note 18).

32. *Argonautica,* II, 1144. One should consult Francis Vian's and Emile Delage's excellent French edition. Paris: Les Belles Lettres (G. Budé), 1976-1981, 3 vol.

33. *Theatrum Chemicum,* t.II, p. 324.

34. *Ibid.,* pp. 357 f.

35. *Ibid.,* p. 358. Sylvain Matton has translated the initial portion of this text (article cited, pp. 9 f.).

35. *Mythologiae sive explicationum fabularum libri decem,* Venice, 1551, cf. Book VI, chap. 7.

37. Jacques Gohory. *Hystoria Jasonis, Thessaliae principis, de colchica velleris aurei expeditione, cum figuris aere excusis earumque expositione, versibus priscorum poetarum, ab Jacobe Gohorio.* Paris, 1563, 26 plates, drawings by Leonard Tiry, engraved by René Boyuin. And *Liuvre de la conqueste de la toison d'or par le prince Iason de Tessalie faict par figures avec exposition d'icelles.* Paris, 1563, same plates. British Library, classification number C.66p.p. 28. I found their alchemical or hermetical inspiration not marked enough to include them among the illustrations presented in this work. On this *Hystoria Jasonis,* cf. François Secret. "Situation de la littérature alchimique en Europe à la fin du XVIème siècle et au début du XVIIème siècle", in *XVIIeme siècle,* nr. CXX, 1978. After relating the story of Jason, Gohory winds up his short text with more personal considerations and mentions Chrysogonus Polydorus' interpretation (who was probably Andreas Osiander): "Navigatio periculosa difficultatem indaganda materie lapilli (ut vocant) Philosophici indicat. Ea, qui telluris vicem obtinet a marte metallorum. Deo, Ager martius appellatur: et quia igne purganda praeparanda et à Tauris ignem spirantibus exaranda et excolenda." On Gohory, cf. D.P. Walker. *Spiritual and demonic magic from Ficino to Campanella.* London: The Warburg Institute; 1958, reed. 1969 (Kraus Reprints) and 1975 (Univ. of Notre Dame Press); French ed: Paris: Albin Michel, 1988. Walker mentions the existence of a doctoral dissertation on Gohory, by Willis Herbert Bowen, Univ. of Harvard (1936). Cf. also: E.T. Hamy. "Un précurseur de Guy de la Brosse: Jacques Gohory et le Lycium philosophal

de Saint-Marceau-lès-Paris (1571-1576)," pp. 1-26, in: *Nouvelles archives du Museum,* fourth series, t.I (1899). And: *Les Bibliothèques françoises de la Croix du Maine et de Du Verdier,* new edition, 1773, t.III, pp. 280 f. (National Library, classification number *Usuels Nationales Françaises* 15).

38. "Chrysorrhoas, sive de arte chimica dialogus", pp. 1-25 in: *Alchemiae, quam vocant, artisque metallicae, doctrina, certusque modus, scriptis tum novis, tum veteribus, duobus Voluminibus comprehensus.* Basel, 1577. Includes thirteen treatises: "Chrysorrhoas" is the first one; this is a dialogue between Chrysophilus and Theophrastus about alchemy. The first edition is dated 1561.

39. Salomon Trismosin. *Aureum Vellus Oder Güldin Schatz- und Kunstkammer.* Rorschach, 1598. Volume II was supposedly published in Basel in 1604. New edition in Hamburg, in 1708; and in 1718 with the title *Eröffnete Geheimnisse des Steins der Weisen oder Schatzkammer der Alchymei.*

40. There is, however, in the second part, a treatise called *Der Güldin Flüss* and ascribed to Paracelsus.

41. Cf. Ferguson, II, 87. Here I refer to the *Theatrum Chemicum* edition (V, 240-428). The book is dedicated to a dignitary of the Order of the Golden Fleece.

42. *Ibid.,* pp. 250 f., cf. also p. 354.

43. *Ibid.,* pp. 251 f. A text by John of Antioch (an author from the sixth-seventh century, already mentioned *supra*), dealing with the repression of the Egyptian revolt in 296 sheds some light on this point: "Diocletian moved against Egypt. Then he made a search for the works written by their ancients on the chemistry of silver and gold, and burnt them, to prevent the Egyptians from obtaining riches from this art and taking advantage of this wealth for competing with the Romans later on." This text is faithfully reproduced by the Suidas (on these testimonies, cf. Robert Halleux, *Alchimistes grecs,* vol. II, "Les Belles Lettres," Paris, forthcoming. I am indebted to him for providing this reference).

44. *Ibid.,* p. 250: "medicinam Jason (id est, medeor, apud Chironem Centaurum viginti annis, ob metum Pelie matrui sui delitescens, atque a puero expositus ibidem educatus) didicisse perhibetur: a Medea autem occultissiman absolutissimamque medendi artem parcepisse." Cf. also pp. 247 ff., f. 354.

45. *Ibid.,* pp. 251 ff.

46. *Ibid.,* p. 254: "Per aratrum adamantinum intelligi vas Hermetis intelligo, per tauros ignivomos materiam in vas conjiciendam in campo Martio seu Marti dicato, quatuor jugerum, hoc est, quatuor elementorum. Dicit enim Hermes: pater ejus est sol, mater ejus Luna, portavit illud ventus in ventre suo, nutrix ejus terra est, et qui ea ignorat, opus non aggrediatur, nam totum erit noxium, infortunium et tristitia: ex ea enim materie imprimis spiritus oriuntur

candidi, qui draconis dentium nuncupatione venire videntur, quique per Jasonis hastam, id est, ignis Philosophici efficaciam interimendi, lapide in medium dentium sive spirituum illorum conjecto: vase firmiter clauso ne fugiant: postremo dracone industria singulari superato, Velleris Aurei copia daretur. Hæc pauca retulisse arcanorum istorum studioso sufficiat."

47. *Ibid.,* p. 246.

48. *Ibid.,* pp. 252-254. Let us also mention a passage from Guidon Pancirol's *Nova Reperta* (Hamburg, t.II, 1602, rendered into Latin by Henricus Salmuth, Paris National Library: classification number Z 19156), in the chapter titled "De Alchymia" (pp. 312-354). This passage deals simultaneously with Hermes Trismegistus, the Emerald Tablet and the Argonauts (pp. 328-331). In Pierre de La Noue's French translation (*Livre premier des Antiquitez perdues,* Lyon, 1617), cf. pp. 214-220.

49. N.p., n.d. Book II, pp. 62-77.

50. *Atalanta Fugiens, hoc est, emblemata nova de secretis naturae chymica.* Oppenheim, 1618. Several reeditions. One should consult the English ed., commented by H.M.E. De Jong (Leyde: Brill, 1969), and the French ed. provided by Etienne Perrot (Paris: Librairie de Médicis, 1969). Cf. also the translation and edition (of the Emblems, Fugues and Epigrams) by Joscelyn Godwin (Grand Rapids, MI: Phanes Press, 1989).

51. "Quin Sobolem Sophiæ sic tripatrem esse ferunt:/Sol etenim primus, Vulcanus at esse secundus/Dicitur, huic præstans tertius arte pater."

52. This point is already well emphasized by H.M.E. De Jong, *op. cit.* pp. 308 f.

53. Cf. *supra,* note 3.

54. *Ibid.,* p. 35. Cf. this text *infra,* Appendix I # 1.

55. *Ibid.,* pp. 586-589.

56. *Chymische Hochzeit Christiani Rosencreutz: Anno 1459.* Strasbourg, 1616. Cf. the German edition provided by Richard Van Dülmen (Stuttgart: Calwer Verlag, 1973, text presented with both "manifestos," the *Fama* and the *Confessio*). French ed: *La Bible des Rose-Croix.* Paris: P.U.F., 1970 (ed. provided by Bernard Gorceix, which also contains both manifestos). Edited and translated into English by Joscelyn Godwin: *The Chemical Wedding of Christian Rosenkreutz* (Grand Rapids, MI, Phanes Press, 1992).

57. Gorceix ed., p. 63. Van Dülmen ed., p. 69: "Eh wir aber uns gesetzt, komment beyde Knaben herein und verehren von dess Brauttigams wegen jedem die Guldin Vliess mit einem fliegenden Löwen; mit begeren, wir wolten dieselbe uber der Tafel anhaben, und dess Ordens, den S.M. uns jetz schenket, bald auch mit gebürlicher weiss erhalten."

58. Gorceix ed., p. 64, note 1. The lion, as well as the ram, is featured on plate XLIX in *Atalanta Fugiens*.

59. Gorceix ed., p. 83. Van Dülmen ed., p. 86

60. Roland Edighoffer. *Rose-Croix et société idéale selon Johann Valentin Andreae*. Paris: Arma Artis, t.I. 1982, pp. 264 ff. T.II, 1987, p. 622.

61. Cf. Thorndike *(History of magic...)*, VIII, pp. 112 f.

62. *La Toyson d'Or, ou la fleur des thrésors...* was reprinted the following year (Ferguson, II, 470, after Gmelin mentions a 1602 edition); cf. also: *Salomon Trismosin: la Toison d'Or ou la fleur des trésors (commentaire des illustrations par Bernard Husson, étude iconographique du manuscrit de Berlin par René Alleau)*. Paris: Retz, 1975.

63. *Ibid.,* pp. 35-42.

64. Cf. Ferguson, II, 31.

65. *Ibid.,* II, 383 and 385. But I could only consult the 1736 edition, with its fine frontispiece engraving representing an alchemical collar and the Golden Fleece as its pendant (cf. figure X). Cf. also *infra,* note 80.

66. Cf. the edition provided by Sylvain Matton: *Les visions hermétiques*. Paris: C.A.L., collection Bibliotheca Hermetica, 1974, pp. 282-285. German edition, *Dreyfaches hermetisches Kleebatt*, 1667. The 1621 French edition is titled: *Traittez de l'harmonie et constitution generalle du vray sel, secret des Philosophes, et de l'Esprit universel du monde, suivant le troisième principe du Cosmopolite*. I have quoted here from this edition.

67. Johann Baptist Großschedel (Equites Romanus, Philochemicus). *Erleuterung des allgewaltigen grossen Buchs der Natur*. Frankfurt/Main: Lucas Jennis, 1629, pp. 80-84 where he recalls the tradition that the "praxis Philosophicum lapidem zu praepariren" is written on a ramskin. The hazardous navigation means the lengthy alchemical studies. Jason narcotizing the dragon signifies that the alchemist sets mercury to rest. And cf. Ferguson, I, 119 and 175.

68. Helmstaedt, 1648, reed. 1669. In the first edition, cf. pp. 25 (1669 ed., p. 27) and 435 ff.: here the Golden Fleece is taken as a parchment.

69. *De Ortu,* pp. 84 ff. (reed. Manget, I, 1. *Hermetis...,* 1674, pp. 53 f., 87 f.).

70. *Vellus Aureum, Das güldene Fluss: Das ist Chymisches Kleinod, Oder Philosophische Beschreibung Der höchsten Medicin, und erquickenden Bronnen dess Lebens Auri Potabilis,* Stuttgart, 1665. I have consulted the copy in the Erlangen-Nuremberg University Library. J.L. Möglin, professor in Tübingen, is also the author of a treatise on palingenesis (cf. Ferguson).

71. The title goes on: *Allen Desselbigen emsigen Bestreitern zur Nachricht darzu zu gelangen; Auss einem Cabalistischen Rätzel erkläret und an den Tag gegeben. Auch mit sonderbaren Anmerckungen und einem dienlichen Anhang aussgefertigt.* 118 pages, pagination incomplete. Consulted copy: Erlangen-Nuremberg University Library.

72. This address to the reader comes after the *Vorbericht* and the *AEnigma cabalistarum.* Here the author provides in a note a Latin translation of the Greek text we know, where the Suidas tells about the Golden Fleece.

73. *Mercure Galant,* December 1679. The picture is between pages 348 and 349. The answer to the quiz is given on pages 295ff. in the January 1680 issue. Two articles are subsequently published in the same paper, within three months, on these subjects: *De la Pierre Philosophale* et *Des feux follets.* Didier Kahn has already pointed to this quiz in the *Mercure Galant,* and given the text of January 1680: cf. Didier Kahn. "L'alchimie sur la scène française aux XVIème et XVIIème siècles", pp. 62–96 in: *Chrysopoeia. Revue publiée par la Société d'Etude et d'Histoire de l'Alchimie,* t.II, fasc. I, January-March 1988, Milan: Arché, and Paris: J.C. Bailly; cf. pp. 67f. In this late seventeenth century, let us also mention the publication of Jacob Tollius' book *Fortuita. In quibus, praeter critica nonnulla, tota fabularis Historia Graeca, Phoenicia, AEgyptiaca, ad Chemiam pertinere asseritur.* Amsterdam, 1687 (on the Golden Fleece, cf. p. 57). And the publication of the anonymous *Dictionnaire Hermétique contenant l'explication des Termes, Fables, Enigmes et manières de parler des vrais Philosophes,* ascribed to Guillaume Salmon, Paris, 1695. In this *Dictionnaire,* we find for instance: "The Golden Fleece safely kept in the Temple of Mars is the matter through which the work of the Stone is accomplished, which is put into an athanor or furnace, this being a fort partly in iron called Mars." The bulls watching over the temple of Mars were sending flames out of their nostrils, which indicates that the fire should be carefully tended and "that the Sages understand the nostrils to be the furnaces' registers." The dragon guarding the Fleece stands for mercury, difficult to put to sleep or rest, difficult to fix. Through Medea's skills it turned from volatile to fixed and to a medicine used by Medea—whose name means "medicine"—to restore AEson to youth (cf. mostly pp. 44f., 203ff.).

74. Cf. Van Lennep, *Alchimie, op. cit. supra,* note 25, p. 238. This reproduction is also found in the edition of the *Visions hermétiques* provided by Sylvain Matton (cf. *supra,* note 35, p. 98).

75. "Kolchis mag sein goldenes Fell und ihr goldenes Vlies behalten" (K.F. von Greiffenberg. "Frühlingslust," in: *Sämtliche Werke in zehn Bänden,* hrsg. von Martin Bircher und Friedhelm Kemp. New York: Kraus Reprint Milwood, 1983, t. VIII., p. 735.

76. Eugène Canseliet. *Deux logis alchimiques (op. cit. supra,* note 22), cf. pp. 37-140. On the Golden Fleece, cf. pp. 114-117, notably for the ms. of the Vatican Library. But, more importantly, cf. Mino Gabriele: a) *Il giardino di*

Hermes. Massimiliano Palombara alchimista et rosacroce nella Roma del Seicento. Rome : Editrice Ianua, 1986, cf. illustrations p. 126 and 132; b) "La Porta del Vello d'Oro: Iconologia e tradizione alchemica," p. 17–27 in : *La Porta Magica. Luoghi e memorie nel giardino di piazza Vittorio,* a cura di Nicoletta Cardano. Rome : Fratelli Palombi Editori, 1990.

77. Cf. Ferguson, I, 363 f.

78. *Xystus in hortum Hesperidum,* 1696 ed., cited by Ferguson, I, 364; the 1715 ed. with its subtitle is cited by Kopp, *op. cit.,* I, 244. I have not been able to consult this work.

79. The title goes on: *Metamorphosis metallorum ignobiliorum in aurum nativo praestantius asserens,* 46 pp., in German and Latin alternately. Consulted copy: Erlangen-Nuremberg Univ. Library, bound with the *Tantalus Chemicus* (1717) by the same author. In the article cited *supra,* note 1, I have mentioned another treatise by Hannemann, *Disputatio Chymica de Hermete Trismegisto,* 1706.

80. *Das Güldene Vliess und der urälteste verborgene Schatz der Weisen, in welchem da ist die allgemeine "materia prima," derselben nothwendige "praeparation" und überaus reiche Frucht des philosophischen Steins augenscheinlich gezeiget.* Leipzig, 1736. The author signs "Ich Sags Nichts" ("I do not say"), and the initial letters might indicate Johann Siebmacher Nirnbergsis. As a matter of fact, the attribution is quite certain. The fine engraving (already mentioned *supra,* note 65) representing the Golden Fleece is signed C.F. Boetius. Fictuld, in *Probierstein* (cf. *infra,* note 105), mentions a 1607 edition, and Ferguson the editions of 1609, 1661, 1736, 1737, 1760. Siebmacher, an alchemist of the beginning of the 17th century in Nuremberg, is also the author of two theosophical "weigelian" (i.e., in the wake of Valentin Weigel) books in 1618. He also signs under the name of Huyldrich Bachsmeier von Regenbrun. On him, see Reinhard Breymayer: "Introduction," in: *Johann Valentin Andreae: Ein geistliches Gemälde. Entworfen und aufgezeichnet von Huldrich StarkMann, Diener des Evangeliums. Nach dem widergefundenen Urdruck Tübingen 1615,* hrsg. von Reinhard Breymayer. Tübingen: Noûs-Verlag Thomas Heck, 1991 (published in 1992), pp. VII ff.

81. Tübingen, 1737. Cf. Ferguson, I, 182f. Published the same year and titled *Ehrenrettung der Alchymie.*

82. Tübingen, 1737. Divided into three sections; the first one is entitled "De Historia Aurei Velleris, et de Principiis Metallorum," etc. Ferguson (I, 183) cites another edition published in 1739. Second edition, in German: *Abhandlung vom goldenen Vliess oder Möglichkeit der Verwandlung der Metalle.* Tübingen, 1787, and the same year in the *Magazin für höhere Naturwissenschaft und Chemie,* t.II, Tübingen, pp. 1ff.

83. Cf. the "Proemium", pp. 7–10. P. 8 on the auriferous rivers.

84. P. 9: "Periculum istud et difficultas superari non potest, neque à summo Imperante abitus ulli conceditur, nisi progeniei unicæ Medeaæ, hoc est, *Sapientiae,* Artiumque omnium Magistrae, ope perficiatur, ut sensum fabulæ omnem sic planissime patere arbitremur."

85.   Pp. 9f.: Philip the Good created his Order "iis quidem temporibus, quibus plura egregia inventa Germaniæ, et præcipue Typographia, orbi innotuerunt. Id quod vel sola quam gestant ordinis hujus summi Equites, aurea demonstrat catena, cujus articuli repræsentant *Chalybem,* qualis ad ignem eliciendum adhibetur, cum *lapide vel silicibus,* e quibus flamma promicat, cum symbolo: *Ante ferit quam flamma micat,* iisque in fine penduale adduntur exuviae agni, seu *Vellus* istud *Aureum,* cum inscriptione: *Pretium non vile laborum,* quo ipso symbolo philosophico impetu animati operam non lusuros nos speramus, si *Dissertatione Academica* excutere conemur igniculos quosdam, qui *Vellus* nobis aureum, hoc est materiam seu argumentum de *Possibilitate mutationis et meliorationis metallorum collustrent.* Faxit aeterna sapientia FELICITER." Also noteworthy at this time the reedition, in German, of Aurelio Augurelli's *Vellus Aureum et Chrysopoeia* (cf. *supra,* note 24), Hamburg, 1716. Of course, "hieroglyphic" readings, other than chemical, are still proposed. For instance, Hermann von der Hardt in his *Aureum Vellus Argonautarum ex Orphei Thesauro* (Helmstedt, 1715, 29 pp.) tries to show that proper nouns are a disguise for town names (Jason means Magnesia, Medea refers to Medeon, etc.), and that the adventures related in this fable conceal in fact historical events somehow fallen into oblivion.

86. Cf. Hermann Kopp's extensive note about him (II, 208–220), partially corrected by Ferguson (II, 130f.). The mention of the Turkish jail, which I found in vol. I, might well give a clue toward some identification.

87. I have consulted the copy in the Munich Bayerische Staatsbibliothek (1733 ed.).

88. *Aureum Vellus oder Güldenes Vliess Das ist, ein Tractat, welcher darstellet den Grund und Ursprung des uhralten güldenen Vliefses, worinnen dasselbe ehemahls bestanden und noch, was eine gefährliche weite Reise deswegen angestellet worden, und von weme, auch wie es endlich zu einer allerhöchsten Ritter—Orden gediehen, durch wen und warum solche billig allen andern Orden wegen ihrer Vortrefflichkeit vorzuziehen, und wie solche unmassgeblich auch in der That zugleich wieder auf den alten Fuss zu restituiren und zu setzen sey, so dass auch das Erstere wieder bey solcher hohen Orden wäre. Und zugleich Deo Gratias, Wegen der biss anhero, vermittelst seiner Göttlichen Gnaden und Seegen, durch die unwiedersprechliche richtige Concordanz der Philosophorum Hermeticorum endlich noch erfundene Wahrheit und Möglichkeit derselben Kunst. Wie auch Ultimum Vale bey der gantzen Welt, in Specie aber all denjenigen, welche biss anhero seine Schrifften werth geachtet, mit dem Versprechen, wo er ein oder den andern bey seinem Leben particulariter noch dienen*

kan, sonderlich denen er nicht volkommene Satisfaction gegeben hätte, sie sich aber gleichwohl höflich aufgeführet, er nichts ermangeln werde; und zugleich einen Beschluss aller seiner nach der Harmonie der Philosophorum herausgegebenen Tractaetgen, so meist in einem kurtzen Begriff ex veris Philosophis sincerè extractum & ipso facto nunc comprobatum, bestehen. Editio Secunda. Cum Supplemento Aurei Velleris vermehret. Franckfurt am Mayn, bey Stocks Seel. Erben und Schilling, 1733. T.I, 60 + 384 pp. T.II, 320 pp.

89. Address to the reader, pp. 51 ff. On the Knights of the Sun and the Rosicrucians, cf. chap. II, p. 570. On the Knight of the Sun as a higher degree in Freemasonry, cf. Pierre Mollier, *Le Chevalier du Soleil : Contribution à l'étude d'un haut-grade maçonnique en France au XVIIIe siècle,* typescript at the E.P.H.E. (Vème Section), Sorbonne, Dissertation 1992.

90. Pp. 1-176.

91. Pp. 245-303.

92. Pp. 7f.

93. Pp. 10f., he also censures Melchior Balthazar Kupperschmid regarding this. The passage about the word "Schaff" is on pp. 170f.

94. Pp. 24f. Naxagoras gives an interesting list of authors, including Johann Hübner, Johann Michael Dillherr, Martin Zeiler, Johann Christoph Nehring, and others.

95. Pp. 25f. What Naxagoras calls *Alchymie Spiegel* is probably Joost Van Balbian's *Speculum Alchemiae,* published circa 1600. In this connection, he also quotes Aloisius Marlianus (cf. *supra,* note 25), altering his spelling (pp. 26, 72). In spite of its obvious interest, Naxagoras' book was written somewhat hastily; thus in various places he quotes passages devoted to the Golden Fleece and ascribes them to Marsilio Ficino, even mentioning the page (pp. 184f.)! Reading the *Dreyfaches Hermetisches Kleeblatt* (cf. *supra,* note 65) enabled me to elucidate this little mystery: at the same time the *Kleeblatt* presents a text by Nuysement, and another by Ficino. Naxagoras gave the right page but not the right author; all that he ascribed to Ficino (in an extensive passage repeated twice) is by Nuysement.

96. Pp. 29f., 32f., 47ff., 74, 166-168. On the figures living an unusually long life, cf. chap. X. The AES itself appears again in the poem, p. 61 of the *Supplementum,* appended to the picture studied by Joachim Telle in *Présence d'Hermès Trismégiste* (cf. *supra,* note 1). Let us remember that this word means "brazen, brass, copper," and also "money, fortune, means." As a matter of fact, philological researches by specialists of Indo-European confirm that all these names for Colchis derive from the name of this metal (Aes, Aies, Aia). In this book, *"Aureum Vellus"* is sometimes a mere synonym for *"tingirender Stein"* (cf. for instance vol. I, p. 276).

97. Pp. 36–40, 80f.

98. Pp. 66–68. On Democrites as an alchemist, cf. Ferguson, I, 205. and Kopp, I, 202–219; II, 319. Seneca was one of the first to give evidence of Democrites' alchemical activity. On the destruction of the books by Diocletian, cf. *supra,* note 43.

99. Pp. 82f.

100. Pp. 158–163, 175f.

101. Franz Kieser, *Cabala Chymica. Concordantia Chymica,* Mulhouse, 1606. Cf. Ferguson, I, 464f., and Bernard Gorceix who has presented, in French translation, some passages from this work, pp. 185–219 in: *Alchimie (traités allemands du XVIeme siècle, traduits et présentés par B. Gorceix).* Paris: Fayard, collection "L'Espace intérieur," 1980. And Naxagoras has also authored a *Sancta Veritas Hermetica, seu Concordantia Philosophorum* (Breslau, 1712; cf. Ferguson, II, 130). It would be interesting to trace the history of this notion of "concordance." A typical case in point is Pietro of Abano's *Conciliator* (1250-circa 1313). Medieval physicians were already developing 'concordanciae' when attempting to reconcile the teachings of Galen, Hippocrates, and Avicenna.

102. Pp. 49f., text repeated pp. 75f. Madathanus (1603–1638), physicist and poet, author of several alchemical treatises, including *Aureum Saeculum Redivivum.*

103. Pp. 298ff.

104. P. 42.

105. Cf. A. Faivre. *Accès de l'Esotérisme occidental* (cited *supra,* note 9), p. 210.

106. Notably in *Hermetica Victoria,* Leipzig, 1750, p. 43; and in *Chymisch-Philosophischer Probierstein,* Frankfurt and Leipzig, 1740, pp. 43 and 105. Naxagoras' book is cited in Fictuld's *Aureum Vellus,* p. 165.

107. *Aureum Vellus Oder Goldenes Vlies. Das ist warhaffte Entdeckung, was dasselbige sey? Sowohl in seinem Ursprung, als auch in seinem erhabenen Zustande; Aus denen Alterthümern hervor gesucht und denen filiis Artis, und Liebhabern der Hermetischen Philosophie, dargeleget, auch, dass darunter die Prima Materia Lapidis Philosophorum, sammt dessen Praxi verborgen, eröffnet, und mit dienlichen Anmerckungen erkläret.* Published pp. 121–379 with *Azoth and Ignis* (pp. 1–120), Leipzig, bei Michael Blockberger, 1749. Consulted copy Munich Bayerische Staatsbibliothek.

108. P. 123.

109. P. 164. Mennens is quoted p. 253. On the 1736 *Golden Vliess,* cf.

supra, note 80.

110. P. 189.

111. Pp. 217ff.

112. Pp. 208 f.

113. P. 142.

114. Cf. *supra,* note 9.

115. Pp. 135f.

116. Pp. 138 and 140.

117. Pp. 169 f.

118. Pp. 184 ff.

119. P. 295.

120. Pp. 299 f.

121. Pp. 300 f.

122. Pp. 302–305.

123. Pp. 307–312. On F. Kieser, cf. *supra,* note 101.

124. Pp. 313.

125. Pp. 316 ff.

126. P. 329.

127. P. 370.

128. *Die Sonne von Osten. Oder philosophische Auslegung der Kette des goldenen Vliesses, nebst dem Kreuze der Ritterorden der Tempelherrn, Johaniter, Teutschherrn, u.a.d. und etwelcher Cabalistischen Figuren samt einem Spiegel oder Probierstein der philosophischen Materie, und einer besonderen Auslegung desselben an seine Freunde der Weissheit Söhne.* Von Rosa Significent Hunnis ea. 5783. (11 + 277 pp.).

129. Cf. *supra,* note 18, on the reedition of the *Fables.* Reed. of the *Dictionnaire:* Milan: Arché, 1969. About Dom Pernety, cf. Micheline Meillassoux-Salmon (*alias* Meillassoux-Le Cerf) *Dom Pernety et son milieu (1715-1796). Contribution à l'histoire de la sensibilité et des idées dans la deuxième moitié du XVIIIe siècle.* Thèse de Doctorat d'État Paris IV—Sorbonne, 1988, 800 pp. Published by Archè (Paris) in 1992.

130. Reed. 1715. The best version is the third ed. (1738-1740). Cf. t.III (1740 ed.), pp. 198 ff.

131. *Ibid.,* p. 200.

132. Pernety, *Fables,* p. 439, t.I, Book 2.

133. *Ibid.,* p. 451.

134. *Ibid.,* p. 484.

135. *Ibid.,* p. 419. Such concern is in evidence throughout the other chapters of this large volume, and of course it is already present in the introduction: what must be found, he says, is "a system through which everything can be explained, down to the minutest details of the facts herein recorded, no matter how odd, how incredible and how conflicting in appearance." He admits that this 'system' is nothing new, but omits mentioning that most of the people who used it were not really content with it (p. 2).

136. *Ibid.,* pp. 440, 449.

137. *Ibid.,* pp. 455 f.

138. *Ibid.,* pp. 456 through 460.

139. *Ibid.,* pp. 464 f.

140. *Ibid.,* p. 470.

141. *Ibid.,* p. 475.

142. *Ibid.,* p. 477.

143. *Ibid.,* p. 478.

144. *Ibid.,* pp. 441 f.

145. "Le chêne qu'on employa à la construction de ce Navire, est le même que celui contre lequel Cadmus tua le serpent qui avoit dévoré ses compagnons; c'est ce chêne creux, au pied duquel étoit planté le rosier d'Abraham Juif, dont parle Flamel; le même encore qui environnoit la fontaine de Trévisan, et celui dont d'Espagnet fait mention au 114e Canon de son Traité. Il faut donc que ce tronc de chêne soit creux; ce qui lui a fait donner le nom de Vaisseau. On a feint aussi que Typhis fût un des Pilotes, parce que le feu est le conducteur de l'œuvre [...] On lui donna Ancée pour adjoint, afin d'indiquer que le feu doit être le même que celui d'une poule qui couve, comme le disent les Philosophes."

146. *Ibid.,* p. 459, for the quotation. This text has refere Nicolas Flamel and Bernard de Trévise. And pp. 210 f. from the *Dictionnaire.*

147. The manuscript of Denis Molinier ("Chevalier de l'Ordre Royal et Militaire du Christ," cf. p. 204 of the ms.) is in the Paris National Library, classification number FR 14 765. It is not exclusively concerned with alchemy, but also offers chapters on sacred numbers, and on the catechisms of the Elus Cohens. For the dates of this manuscript, cf. p. 333 (year 1773) and pp. 194 f.

(year 1778). Passages relating to the Golden Fleece are pp. 27–30, 33f., 232. Jacques Van Lennep has published several drawings from this ms. in *Alchimie* (cf. *supra,* note 26): refer to the index of *Alchimie.*

148. "Jason (…) consulte la médecine de l'enchanteresse Medée parce qu'il est tout naturel que le (Soufre) de nature *personnifié dans Jason* cherche l'autre moitié de luy même (Mercure) pour vaincre les difficultés qu'il doit rencontrer pour sa perfection et pour devenir élixir (…) ainsi Jason sort de Medée et tous les deux l'amant et la metresse ne font qu'une seule chose pour accomplir nôtre oeuvre en se réunissant en Elixir. Cependant pour déclarer nôtre secret sans réserve il est bon de vous avertir que cet amant et cette maitresse, ce mâle et cette femelle, sont eux-mêmes composés de plusieurs substances et qu'ils ont été formés pare diverses opérations de nôtre art (…) Jason est également un esprit de (Soufre) ainsy que Persée mais beaucoup plus parfait que luy, car celuy cy est aussy fixe que l'autre est volatil et quiquonque en veut jouir doit recourir a Minerve Mère de la science et a Medée compagne de l'expérience, car il faut une Industrie, très consommée pour unir des esprits et les joindre par un traité de mariage éternel afin qu'ils se convertissent en (Soufre) fixe et permanant qui est appelé pierre des philosophes ou la toyson d'Or, remportée par Jason (…) Nous entendons par Médée ce (Soufre) de nature de la troisième espèce parce qu'alors il est nôtre Medée c'est-à-dire Médecine propre à toutes les maladies et par conséquant la clef de toute la médecine, ou magie naturelle et le fondement de la religion, et de la Cabale dont nous avons déja dit de grandes choses (…)." In the same moment, and in a reductionistic way reminiscent of Dom Pernety, Libois writes in his *Histoire mythologique ou Encyclopédie des Dieux et des héros de la Fable* (Paris, 1773; 2nd edition, 1776) : "Le voyage des Argonautes, dont Jason est le chef, n'est autre chose qu'un point de physique, qui se fait dans la nature par la mutation des qualités des élémens, pour en composer un corps, et en le dépouillant de tout ce qu'il a de terrestre, le rendre simple et spirituel, de terrestre qu'il étoit […] Tous les noms des Argonautes ne sont que des qualités prises des élémens du feu, de l'eau et de la terre produites à l'air, afin d'y aquérir la simplicité" (p. 304 s, ed. 1776).

149. Louis-Claude de Saint-Martin. *Tableau Naturel des rapports qui unissent Dieu, l'homme et l'univers.* Paris, 1782, vol. I. Cf. pp. 210–220.

150. Franz von Baader. *Revision der Philosopheme der Hegel'schen Schule* (1839), edited in the *Sämtliche Werke,* t. IX, cf. pp. 380 s.

151. Let us mention at least the vast plagiary signed M.A. de Nantes (*Clef des oeuvres de Saint Jean et de M. de Nostredame,* n.p., n.d. 1871, facsimile reedition Neuilly: Arma Artis, 1983), where we find (without references or even brackets) extensive passages from Pernety's *Fables.* The chapter entitled "Historie de la conquête de la Toison d'Or," p. 177–184, in M.A. de Nantes' book, is a word-for-word copy of pp. 457–474 of Pernety's *Fables,* t.I, Book 2; the plagiary has merely suppressed Pernety's references to alchemic authors. This being said, some passages in this book, devoted to other topics, are not devoid of

interest.

152. On Fulcanelli's personality, cf. André Van den Broeck's recent book. *Al-Kemi:Hermetic, Occult, Political, and Private Aspects of R.A. Schwaller de Lubicz.* Rochester: Vermont: Inner Traditions International, 1987, 287 pp. For a different approach, cf. Kenneth Rayner Johnson. *The Fulcanelli Phenomenon.* Jersey: Neville Spearman, 1980, IX and 323 pp.

153. Cf. *supra,* note 24, and figure IV.

154. 1964 edition, pp. 194f.

155. *Ibid.,* pp. 196f.

156. *Ibid.,* pp. 197f.

157. Cf. the two works cited notes 23 (*Deux logis alchimiques*) and 158 (*Alchimie*), names index, "Golden Fleece."

158. It was published in 1936 in the review *Atlantis,* and reprinted in *Alchimie: Etudes diverses de symbolisme hermétique et de pratique philosophale.* Paris: Pauvert, 1964, reed. 1978, cf. pp. 195–239. The following references refer to this second edition.

159. *Ibid.,* pp. 195f.

160. *Ibid.,* p. 208 "De même voit-on, au cours du travail alchimique, la partie pure du composé se séparer de la masse putréfiée, s'éloigner de tout danger et s'élever à la surface, véhiculée par un corps nouveau, de complexion subtile et semblable à elle sous le rapport de la perfection. C'est ainsi qu'Hermès, dans sa *Table Smaragdine,* s'adresse au *fils de science* et lui conseille d'opérer: 'Tu sépareras la terre du feu, le subtil de l'épais, doucement, avec grande industrie."

161. *Ibid.,* p. 232. "Au reste, nous n'aurions pas cru devoir reprendre la longue et minutieuse explication que Dom Antoine-Joseph Pernety fournit dans ses deux savants volumes sur le périple du navire *Argo.* La voie *humide* suivie par l'érudit Bénédictin, au cours de cette *périlleuse navigation,* offre cependant de remarquables analogies avec la *voie brève* dont les Adeptes se montrent si jaloux et qu'ils voilent très souvent sous la première."

162. "Selon que l'exige l'authentique noblesse, les armoiries de Jean Bourré naissent ici de la dépouille du bélier à toison d'or, que l'image montre toute fraîche conquise. L'esprit du monde, dont la laine magique attire le magnétisme et le recueille en elle, se retrouve et zigzague sur le champ de l'écu. / C'est la même projection qui tombe de l'espace et qui sature les linges étendus au printemps par le couple du *livre sans paroles* ou Mutus Liber."

163. *Deux logis alchimiques,* op. cit., pp. 185 and 115–117.

164. Cf. René Roux. *Le Problème des Argonautes. Recherches sur les*

aspects religieux de la légende. Paris: Ed. de Boccard, 1949. As far as I know this is the best work on the symbology of the Golden Fleece, with a remarkable and well-researched approach to its imagery. The author has left aside medieval and modern exegeses, including alchemy. Although restricted to the Greek myth proper, this study constitutes the most stimulating approach to it. The comparison with Puss in Boots is on p. 318. Also to be consulted: Max Célérier. *Regards sur la symbolique de la Toison d'Or.* France: Les Editions du Bien Public, 1990. This is a book of lesser scope than Roux', and besides not much concerned with alchemy. However, it has some very interesting comments on the symbology of the bestiary related to this myth, together with its various episodes.

165. R. Roux, op. cit., p. 252.

166. *Ibid.,* pp. 267 ff., 291. On the tabernacle, cf. *Exodus* 26:14; 39:34.

167. *Argonautica,* IV, 124. French translation by Emile Delage and Francis Vian. Paris: Les Belles Lettres (Budé), t.III, p. 74.

168. *Ibid.,* t.I, 1976, p. 84. *Argonautica,* I, 725-729. Compare with the "flame-like" reflection of the Fleece upon Jason's face (IV, 173); on the tunic given to Apsyrtos, cf. IV, 424; on the tunic worn by Medea during her magical operations, IV, 1661.

169. Cf. *Ibid.,* t.I, p. 84, note 1.

170. *Ibid.,* t.I, p. 77 (*Argonautica,* IV, 167-182). Cf. also *supra,* note 76, about the 'skin of the King' and the Gate of the Palombara villa.

171. Cf. Virgil's *Georgica,* III, 391; Pan captures the moon "munere niveæ lunæ."

172. According to Pausanias, quoted by R. Roux, *op. cit.,* p. 263.

173. Hermann Lambeck. *De Mercurii Statua vulgo Iasonis habita.* Thorun, 1861: the author shows how ancient representations of Jason putting his sandal back on (and forgetting the other one) are almost a perfect replica of Mercury's similar gesture.

174. R. Roux, *op. cit.,* pp. 285 and 289. Regarding Athena, Max Célérier (*op. cit.,* p. 40) aptly reminds us that this goddess with shining eyes, associated with the construction of Argo and mentioned in connection with the Symplegades, has been symbolized by the owl (for she can see in the darkness of night, or ignorance). A very suggestive picture, which is in the Armorial of the Golden Fleece (Municipal Library, Dijon, and reproduced by Célérier, p. 41), shows this bird covered with the Golden Fleece. The owl is well-known in esoteric or alchemical writings (for instance in Khunrath's *Amphitheatrum Sapientiae Aeternae,* 1609).

175. An alchemist carrying such a scroll is featured on a drawing, itself

part of one of the handwritten and painted scrolls ascribed to the alchemist George Ripley (circa 1415-1490) and called the "Ripley Scrowles" (fifteenth-sixteenth centuries). Cf. Jacques Van Lennep. *Alchimie* (referred to *supra,* note 26), 1985 ed., pp. 91-94, notably illustration 106, p. 93.

176. Cf. *supra,* notes 76 and 170.

177. "Die Helden des Altertums / Ermangeln des Ruhms / Wo und wie er auch prangt, / Wenn sie das golden Vliess erlangt, / Ihr die Kabiren" (verses 8212 ff.).

178. This study is concerned with alchemy, but of course the myth of the Golden Fleece, especially the journey of the Argonauts, when used in initiatory accounts, goes far beyond the realm of alchemy. In the literary field we may quote, for instance, Elisabeth Langgässer's fine novel, *Märkische Argonauten-fahrt* (1950), where the quest is the central theme—which is not the case in the two-part drama by the Austrian Franz Grillparzer, *Das Goldene Vliess* (1820), a masterpiece of the German literature nonetheless. Let us note in this regard that some of the greatest creators, even those who were mystically-minded, have hardly been inclined to take Jason as a man on a spiritual quest or as someone fit for initiation. Dante places him in his inferno (cf. Canto XVIII), where he reduces him to the role of a sinful seducer.

Bibliography

Including books from the Renaissance onward in which the myth of the Golden Fleece is not simply mentioned but appears as part of the title or is commented upon or illustrated through engravings.

1) Works in which the myth is presented only as an allegory of the alchemical or mystical journey:

AUGURELLI (Giovanni Aurelio). *Chrysopœia,* and *Vellus Aureum.* Venice, 1515. Reeditions in *Theatrum Chemicum,* t. III, 1659, p. 197, and in *Bibliotheca Chemica Curiosa* by Manget, t. II, 1702, p. 371.

GOHORY (Jacques). *Hystoria Jasonis Thessaliae Principis de Colchida Velleris aurei expeditione.* Paris, 1553. French edition same year. Work indirectly inspired by alchemy.

L.I., preface to *La Toyson d'Or, ou la Fleur des Thrésors en laquelle est succintement et méthodiquement traité de la Pierre des Philosophes, de son excellence, effets et vertus admirables.* Paris: 1612. New edition: Paris: Retz, collection "Bibliotheca Hermetica," 1975.

GROβSCHEDEL von AICHA. *Erläuterung des allgewaltigen grossen Buchs der Natur.* Frankfurt/Main, 1629,

2) Works in which the myth appears only on the title page:

Aureum Vellus Oder Güldin Schatz- und Kunstkammer. Rorschach, 1598. A selection of alchemical texts.

SIEBMACHER (Johann). *Das Güldene Vliess oder das Allerhöchste, edelste, kunstreichste Kleinod, und der urälteste verborgene Schatz der Weisen.* Published anonymously. Frankfurt, 1609. Several editions.

MOEGLIN (Johann Ludwig). *Vellus Aureum, Das güldene Fluss; das ist Chymisches Kleinod oder philosophische Beschreibung der höchsten Medicin, und erquikenden Bronnen dess Lebens Auri potabilis.* Stuttgart, 1665.

De MONTE HERMETIS (Johann). *Explicatio Centri in Trigono Centri per Somnium, das ist: Erläuterung dess Hermetischen Güldenen Fluss.* Ulm, 1680. A quite rare book. Consulted copy: Oskar Schlag Library, Zurich.

HANNEMANN (Johann Ludovicus). *Jason, seu catalogus testimoniorum veritatis metamorphosin metallorum ignobiliorum in aurum nativo praestantius asserens.* Kiel, 1709. And *Xtus in hortum Hesperidum, i.e., Parasceve ad aureum Vellus.* Keil, 1715

3) Works in which the myth is interpreted only as an allegory of the processes of metals transmutation:

PICO DELLA MIRANDOLA (Gianfrancesco). *De Auro libri tres.* Venice, 1586 (written about 1528). Reedited in *Theatrum Chemicum,* t. II, 1659, p. 312, and in Manget's *Bibliotheca Chemica Curiosa,* t. II, 1702, p. 558.

"Chrysorrhoas, sive de arte chemica dialogus," in: *Alchemiae quam vocant, artisque metallicae, doctrina,* Basel, 1561. Reedited 1577 (cf. p. 1-25), and in *Theatrum Chemicum,* II, 1659, p. 139 s.

NUYSEMENT (Clovis Hesteau, sieur de). *Traittez de l'Harmonie et constitution generalle du vray Sel, secret des Philosophes, et de l'Esprit universelle du monde, suivant le troisième Principe du Cosmopolite.* Paris, 1621. New edition by Sylvain Matton, Paris: Retz, collection "Bibliotheca Hermetica," 1974.

PERNETY (Dom Antoine-Joseph). *Les Fables Égyptiennes et Grecques dévoilées et réduites au même principe, avec une explication des hiéroglyphes, et de la Guerre de Troye.* Paris: 1758. Reproduced in facsimile: Milan: Archè, 1971. Reedited in 1786, reproduced in facsimile: Paris: La Table d'Émeraude, 1980, with an introductory text by Sylvain Matton. On the Golden Fleece, cf. t. I, pp. 437-493.

MOLINIER (Denis). Unpublished commentary on Abraham the Jew's *Livre des figures hiéroglyphiques* (a legendary book ascribed to Nicolas Flamel). Paris National Library, classification number FR 14765. Cf. mostly fol. 27-30, 33s, 232.

4) Works in which the myth is subject to hermeneutical elaborations:

MENNENS (Guilielmus). *Aurei Velleris sive sacrae Philosophiae Vatum selectae ac unicae misteriorumque ac Dei, Naturae et Artis admirabilium, libri tres.* Antwerp 1604. Reedited in *Theatrum Chemicum,* t.

V, 1660, p. 240.

MAIER (Michael). *Arcana Arcanissima, hoc est Hieroglyphica AEgyptio-Graeca, Vulgo necdum cognita, ad demonstrandam falsorum apud antiquas deorum, dearum, heroum, animantium et institutorum pro sacris receptorum, originem.* n.p., n.d. (Oppenheim, circa 1610). *Atalanta Fugiens, hoc est, Emblemata Nova de Secretis Naturae Chymica, Accomodata partim oculis et intellectui, figuris cupro incisis.* Oppenheim, 1617. And: *Symbola Aureae Mensae duodecim Nationum. Hoc est, Hermaea seu Mercurii Festa ab Heroibus duodenis selectis, artis Chymicae usu.* Frankfurt, 1617. New edition in facsimile: Graz: Akademische Druck- und Verlagsanstalt, 1972, with an introductory text by Karl R.H. Frick.

ANDREAE (Johann Valentin). *Chymische Hochzeit Christiani Rosencreütz: Anno 1459.* Strasbourg, 1617. New edition of this novel, provided by Richard Van Dülmen: Stuttgart: Calwer Verlag, 1973. Edited and translated into English by Joscelyn Godwin: *The Chemical Wedding of Christian Rosenkreutz,* Grand Rapids, MI, Phanes Press, 1992.

CREILING (Johann Conrad). *Dissertatio Academica de Aureo Vellere, aut possibilitate transmutationis metallorum.* Tübingen, 1737.

NAXAGORAS (Ehrd of). *Aureum Vellus, oder Güldenes Vliess: Das ist, ein Tractat, welcher darstellet den Grund und Ursprung des uhralten güldenen Vliesses, worinnen dasselbe ehemals bestanden und noch, was vor eine gefährliche weite Reise deswegen angestellet worden.* Frankfurt, 1731–1733, 2 vol.

FICTULD (Hermann). *Aureum Vellus oder Güldenes Vlies. Das ist wahrhaffte Entdeckung, was dasselbe sey? Sowohl in seinem Urspung, als auch in seinem erhahenen Zustande.* Leipzig, 1749.

Die Sonne von Osten, oder philosophische Auslegung der Kette des goldenen Vliesses nebst dem Kreuze der Ritteroden. n.p. 1783. A quite rare book. Consulted copy: Oskar Schlag Library, Zurich.

FULCANELLI. *Le Mystère des cathédrales et l'interprétation ésotérique des symboles hermétiques du Grand Œuvre.* Paris, 1925. Reedited in 1964 (cf. pp. 193–198).

CANSELIET (Eugène). "La Toison d'Or", in: *Atlantis,* June 1936. New edition in: *Alchimie.* Paris, 1964. And, by the same: *Deux Logis alchimiques.* Paris, 1979 (on the Palombara villa and the mansion of Le Plessis-Bourré).

5) The Golden Fleece as shown in drawings and plates illustrating alchemical works:

GOHORY (Jacques). *Hystoria Jasonis, op. cit. supra,* section 1. Léonard Tiry's drawings, cut by René Boyuin, are only indirectly inspired by alchemy.

Speculum Veritatis, early seventeenth century, Latin ms 7289, Vatican Library (drawings reprinted several times in the twentieth century).

MAIER (Michael). *Atalanta Fugiens, op. cit. supra,* section 4, cf. plate 49 (combining the myths of Jason and Orion).

VAN HELPEN (Barnet Coenders). *Escalier des Sages, ou la Philosophie des Anciens. Avec de belles Figures, Par un amateur de la Vérité.* Groningen, 1686. Cf. the plate "Ignis Philosophorum."

SIEBMACHER (Johann). *Das Güldne Vliess, op. cit. supra,* section 2. Cf. the frontispiece of the 1736 Leipzig edition (or does it appear earlier?).

Die Sonne von Osten, op. cit. supra, section 4. Cf. the frontispiece.

FULCANELLI. *Le Mystère des cathédrales, op. cit. supra,* section 4. Cf. p. 98 (the Golden Fleece on a bas-relief in the Hôtel Lallemant).

CANSELIET (Eugene). *Deux Logis alchimiques, op. cit. supra,* section 4. Cf. p. 197 (Jean Bourré's blazon).

Illustrations

FIGURE I

A Florentine Picture Chronicle, being a Series of ninety-nine Drawings representing scenes and personages of Ancient History Sacred and Profane, by Maso Finiguerra. Reproduced from the originals in the British Museum by the Imperial Press, Berlin, with a critical and descriptive text by Sidney Colvin. London: Bernard Quaritch, 1898. These works were made in Florence about the mid-fifteenth century. Hermes Trismegistus and Zoroaster are also protrayed in this series, which is therefore not devoid of hermetic elements. Cf. *Présence d'Hermès Trismégiste,* collective work, edited by A. Faivre. Paris, Albin Michel, collection "Cahiers de l'Hermétisme," 1989, pp. 51 and 59. And A. Faivre, *The Eternal Hermes,* Phanes Press (forthcoming).

125

FIGURE II

FIG. 92.—JASON AND MEDEA.
From a Florentine fifteenth-century Engraving.

A Florentine Picture Chronicle (cf. reference to the legend showed *supra*).
Sidney Colvin believes that this locket, which does not belong to the Finiguerra
series, is from one of his pupils and probably designed to adorn a box or a
basket.

126

FIGURE III

Messire Jean Bourré du Plessis, Louis XI's Superintendent of Finance, has inscribed his blazon upon the ram's skin. This work is found in his Plessis-Bourré mansion. Eugène Canseliet has presented and commented upon this work in *Deux Logis alchimiques. En marge de la science et de l'histoire.* Paris, 1979 (rights reserved): cf. plate XXI, p. 196.

FIGURE IV

Bas-relief from the Chapel of the Hôtel Lallemant, in Bourges. This Hôtel, constructed from 1487 to 1518 by Jean Lallemant, contains many designs inspired by the Great Work. Center left lies the ram's skin, watched over by a threatening dragon seen in profile. Fulcanelli has presented and commented upon this bas-relief in *Le Mystère des Cathédrales,* Paris, 1925. 1964 ed., J.J. Pauvert, cf. p. 194 (rights reserved).

FIGURE V

Recueil de toutes les festes et chapitres du Noble Ordre de la Thoison d'Or depuis la première Institution jusques au temps présent, 1587. Royal Library of Belgium, classification number *Ms 0.454. Two striking images (in color), one with the fleece lying on the grass and receiving the 'shower' of a celestial cloud (cf. Mutus Liber,* an of course Gedeon's fleece); the other with a lion wearing the collar of the Order and a helmet of armour surmounted by a three-branched fleur-de-lis; he carries a gun in his right paw and a flintstone in the left one (on this association of the Fleece and the Lion, cf. notably J.V. Andreae, *Chymische Hochzeit Christiani Rosencreütz,* 1616). I am indebted to Mr. Christian Balister, of the Royal Library, for kindly bringing this work to my attention.

FIGURE VI

From *Speculum Veritatis,* early seventeenth century, Latin MS 7286, Vatican Library. The first of these illustrations, which are pen-and-ink drawings, features a warrior with a wooden leg (Vulcan), carrying in his left arm a sphere bearing the number twelve (that of alchemical operations) and surmounted with a cross. The latter is connected through an arrow to a ram, to which is affixed number thirty-two. Of course, this may simply be the astrological sign Aries, which corresponds to the beginning of the work to be carried out. However, as Jacques Van Lennep, the editor of this series, points out, it would more probably symbolize the sulphur perfected through red-hot heating, or even the matter of the great work itself, symbolized by the Golden Fleece (cf. Jacques Van Lennep. *Alchimie (Contribution à l'histoire de l'Art alchimique).* Brussels and Paris, Crédit Communal de Belgique, and Dervy-Livres, 1985 (2nd edition, pp. 129 ff.).

130

FIGURE VII

Michael Maier. *Atalanta Fugiens, hoc est, emblemata nova de secretis naturae chymica.* Oppenheim, 1618. We read in the epigram, "Of three fathers also the child of wisdom is born / The sun is the first, and Vulcan the second; / the man adept in his art is the third father." This is a representation of the myth of Orion, but in the commentary following the epigram, Maier suggests that he tells about both myths at the same time; and above, in his commentary to emblem forty-four, he includes Jason among the mythological figures symbolizing Alchemy, along with Hercules, Ulysses, Theseus, and Pirithous.

FIGURE VIII

Frontispiece of Amounet de Mailly's work: *Les Mystères de la Toison d'Or.*
Brussels, 1658, in bilingual edition, French and Latin. In spite of the title, there is
no esotericism or alchemy in this book, but the only illustration, this
frontispiece, is suggestive and original enough to find a place beside the two
"alchemical collars" of the next century (cf. *infra,* figures X and XI). The author
writes: "So, after he considered this sacred Order as principle of grace, the Cross
of Saint Andrew, here, was like the tabernacle of the old Law, which was covered
with skins tinted in crimson, *pellibus rubricatis,* a representation of the
Golden Fleece, the order of the Apocalypse requests that we introduce it as a
principle of honor . . . ". Used copy: Municipal Library of Rouen.

132

FIGURE IX

Barent Coenders Van Helpen. *Escalier des Sages, ou Thrésor de la Philosophie.* Cologne, 1693 (1st edition, Groningen, 1686). Illustrated with copper-plate engravings, thirteen of which borrow their subject from mythology. The engraving shown here is devoted to Fire (*Ignis Phm,* that is, *Ignis Philosophorum*). A warrior hands to Hades a gulliverized sheep. Jacques Van Lennep has published this drawing in *Alchimie (op. cit. supra,* cf. figure VI), p. 238, and like him we can see this as Jason offering the conquered Golden Fleece. The ship lying at anchor nearby would be Argo. The acrostic *In Gehenna Nostrae Ignis Scientia* would refer to the dragon watching, in Colchis, over the Fleece which, then, represents the fire that must be overcome or conquered by the alchemist.

133

FIGURE X

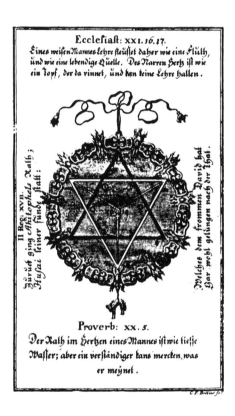

Illustration and title-page of Johann Siebmacher's work (who signs "Ich Sags Nicht"), *Das Güldne Vliess*, 1736 edition. The first edition of the book was issued in 1609, but the drawing is probably contemporaneous with the 1736 edition. Note, beside the collar of pearls with its ram (chivalric Order of the Golden Fleece), the knots in lovelaces (this design is not just an ornament?), together with the peculiar distribution of the planetary signs inside the six-pointed star. This drawing deserves a thorough exegesis.

134

FIGURE XI

Die
Sonne von Osten
Oder
Philofophifche
Auslegung
der
Kette
des
goldenen Bliesses
nebst dem
Kreuze der Ritterorden
der
Tempelherrn, Johanniter,
Teutfchenherrn, u. a. b.
und etwelcher
Cabalistischen Figuren
famt einem
Spiegel oder Probierstein der philosophischen Materie, und einer besonderen
Auslegung desselben
an
feine Freunde der Weisheit Söhne
von
Rofa Significer Hunnis ea,
1 7 8 3.

Illustration on the title-page of the extremely rare alchemical work *Die Sonne von Osten,* published in 1783; as far as I am aware, the only one, with the 1736 work, to give a graphic representation of the Order's collar. We notice the design linking the ram to the collar itself: an eight-petalled flower, the animal being the eighth one (according to a widespread tradition, the number of Christ); at the center, the septenary, looking like a small starry sky. I am indebted to Oskar Schlag for telling me about this book and for lending me his own copy.

Index of Names

137